HALLELUJAH ANYHOW

Victoria A. Eckstein

PublishAmerica
Baltimore

First printing

ISBN: 1-4137-0657-6
PUBLISHED BY
PUBLISHAMERICA, LLLP.
www.publishamerica.com
Baltimore

Printed in the United States of America

DEDICATION

This book is dedicated first and foremost to God. Thank you for everything you have done, are now doing, and will do for me in the future. This is also dedicated to my late father, Robert Lezeene Eckstein. This book is a tribute to my mother, Emily Theresa Eckstein, who has been a source of strength and guidance throughout my life. To my children, Monique Amelia Santiago, and Nicole Shannon Santiago, for their patience and love as I continue to sift through my mess. To my grandchild, Farrah Imani Elder, for her loving spirit and motivation for Grandma. To my sister, Sharon Lezeene Winding, who has been my best friend and spiritual companion. To Pastor Howard John Wesley, and his wife Debbie, for his spiritual guidance and her welcoming spirit. To my coworkers: Tunisia Ezell, Jason Franklin, Rashelle Poirer, Michael Booker, Paulette Tate-Sparks and Zoy Soulis for their positive feedback and assistance throughout this endeavor. To Ricky Thomas for his motivation for this project and for his love and everlasting friendship. And lastly, this book is dedicated to all of the men in my life who have helped to shape, strengthen and mold me into a stronger, wiser person.

Prelude

So, You Think You're Alone

"YOU AIN'T THE FIRST, and you sho'nuff won't be the last." That's one of those old clichés that your mother and grandmother used to say. At the time, it did not alleviate your pain. But, as you got a little older, and have had more of life's experiences, this cliché begins to bring some comfort.

What exactly is that old saying supposed to mean? I mean, really! When you are in the middle of a bad situation, or are suffering from any of the following issues:

heartache,
shame,
pain,
hopelessness,
embarrassment,
depression,
etc.

Who cares about anybody else and what they have to endure. What's real to you is your pain, your trial, your anguish, your heartache. All you can think about is your own stuff, right? You can't possibly imagine anybody else feeling as bad as you do.

Why not? Because your pain is real to you and everybody has a different threshold for the type of pain they can endure.

If you actually believe no one can understand your pain or walk in your shoes—allow me to provide you with something called a testimony...

Chapter One

Be Careful What You Pray For

IT WAS THE LATTER part of September and the seasons were beginning to change. It had been an exceptionally hot summer. I understood we were in store for a very cold winter. Nevertheless, it was a happy time for me. I was preparing for one of the biggest events in my life.

The tensions associated with wedding preparations had subsided significantly. Most everything had been paid for. Premarital counseling with the church pastor had just been completed along with the purchase of garments to be worn. It was to be a simple ceremony, a little less traditional than others. I had spent a considerable amount of time creating centerpieces for the reception tables, along with making the bouquets to be carried.

Everything appeared to be beautifully in sync and anticipation was great. As the day grew nearer, coworkers were all abuzz about the outfits they had purchased to wear at the wedding. Family members talked about who was coming from out of town and how they looked forward to seeing aunt so and so or uncle what's his name.

This particular Saturday evening, I was to attend an event with a coworker. The event turned out to be a surprise bridal shower, put together by my coworkers. The event was wonderful and I smiled so much it hurt my face. Coworkers had blessed us with so many things, such as a limousine for that day to an eight-day honeymoon. The irony is that none of these people were slated to be in the wedding ceremony itself. They were just happy for me.

At night's end, I went home with a car trunk filled with gifts and cards. When I arrived at home, my groom-to-be was not at home. As a matter of fact, no one was home. It was just little ol' me, sitting in the house, taking the time and the peace of the moment to carefully read my cards and view my gifts one more time before I put them in their proper places.

Prior to this night, I was pretty close to canceling the wedding. Despite the fact that the invitations had come back with responses, that preparations had been made, that people were excited; my spirit was nagging me. My past had taught me, oh, so well, that marriage does not magically make issues go away or get better. As a matter of fact, they usually got worse.

My own life's experiences had taught me (the hard way) what kind of commitment it took to make a marriage work. I had been addicted to the day, to the ceremony, not caring about the rest. Life's lessons had taught me about the complexities of marriage. This is the first time I had actually considered the seriousness of committing yourself to another human being, and all of their frailties, forever.

Just last night, I made a determination that I was definitely going to make an announcement soon that the wedding was going to be postponed. It didn't matter about the possible embarrassment or questions that may arise, or even the money that could be lost. It just didn't matter. After the surprise bridal shower, confusion and reluctance were beginning to tug at me. It's not that I wasn't going to postpone the wedding, my struggle was when and how.

Residing in the home at this time, were myself, my 18-year-old daughter, Nicole, and my fiancé, Jerome. Prior to my leaving for the bridal shower, he and I had a small disagreement. We argued about him taking my brand-new, red, shiny Subaru Forester while I was gone.

You see, I did not want him taking my car to go hang out at places I did not particularly care for. This had been a BIG problem for us in our relationship and I had a gut feeling he was "up to no good."

Meaning, our relationship was pretty solid, except for one major area. Jerome had a tendency to go out to strip clubs and bars, get high or intoxicated and then come home the next morning. These behaviors had decreased significantly over the past three some odd years, but it was a source of constant disruption in our relationship.

Jerome had been kicked out of the house more times than I can count. He had gotten so used to being kicked out, he began to pack his own bags after a night of partying or whatever else, without hearing a word out of my mouth. He just looked at me and began packing his things, stating, "I know, I know, get out, right?" I would hold out my hand for the keys to the house and car and would leave the room while he packed.

I had been struggling with a variety of mixed emotions and thoughts. In one sense, I knew Jerome was the man I was destined to marry. I wrestled with this nagging thought that the timing was off. I had been praying for God to give me the answers I needed. I had prayed for God to do something to get Jerome to stop his self-destructive behaviors.

Despite his flaws, Jerome was a wonderful man, with many gifts and talents. He knew God and had a wonderful heart. He had one foot into serving God and the other foot into his old lifestyle. He constantly struggled with being a Christian man and being a man who was used to giving into his fleshly desires.

When I came home that night and saw that my fiancé was not there, I knew that this was my way out. I knew not to expect to see or hear from him until the early morning hours and I was ready to get myself a good night's rest. I would deal with him in the morning.

For tonight, I just wanted to bask in the moment. I wanted to enjoy the thoughtfulness of my family and friends. I carefully looked at each gift and card. I made sure I knew who gave me which gift. I knew they would have to be returned.

I had already drafted a brief letter to all the invitees to the wedding. The letter was simply stating that the wedding had been postponed. I had written the letter two months ago. There was no particular event that triggered this letter. I just knew I would need it at some point.

That night, before turning in, I read my favorite biblical scripture. It was Proverbs 3:5 & 6. This scripture simply states, "Trust in the Lord with all your heart. Lean not unto your own understanding. Seek God's will in everything you do and He will direct your paths." I strongly believed in the power of that scripture. It had become a guide for my entire life. I prayed a simple prayer and told God that I put all my trust in Him and whatever His will was, then I was willing to accept it.

I slept soundly most of the night, but was awakened abruptly at 4:00 in the morning. Something did not feel right. Once I was fully awake, I noticed Jerome had not come home yet. I could feel the anger welling up inside of me. I began pacing the floor, imagining he were in the room. I pretended I was cursing him out. I was preparing my speech for when he returned.

After about an hour of pacing and smoking cigarettes, I decided to go back to bed. "Whatever!" I slept for another two hours and woke up at 7:00 a.m. He was not home yet!!! I was heated!!! There was more pacing, more smoking, and more imaginary cursing-out sessions.

I got myself dressed and began cleaning the house. This was

my normal routine for a Sunday morning. I watched Bishop T.D. Jakes on television, hoping to get some message or word that would help calm me down. I was looking for something to give me the guidance and wisdom to know how to handle this situation. It never came.

It was now 7:30 a.m. and I was deciding whether or not I was going to go to the 8:00 church service or the 11:00 service. I usually never let anything interrupt my attendance at church. But today was different. I felt I needed to wait for him, to deal with this issue immediately. Something felt really, really wrong.

Finally, at 8:30 a.m. the telephone rang. I knew it was him. I did not even look at the caller ID to see where he was calling from. I just reached for the phone and stated, "Hello," in the nastiest tone I could muster.

Just as I expected, it was his voice on the other end. The conversation was brief. "Vic, it's me."

"Oh yeah. What do you want?"

"Listen to me, Vic."

"Go ahead."

"I'm in jail."

"In jail! For what? What now?"

"You won't believe this one."

"Try me."

"They're charging me with rape."

"What did you say?"

"You heard me. Let me explain."

"Explain! Are you crazy? Rape! Don't you ever call me again."

"Wait, Vic. Don't hang up. Let me expl—"

SLAM.

Chapter Two

Sins of the Father

AS A CHILD MY life was saturated with chaos. Therefore, the chaos in my adult life was not really a surprise. I was raised in a two-parent household. I had an older brother, Ricky, a younger brother, Chris, and a younger sister, TC. My father was addicted to heroin and had all the dysfunctional behaviors that come with such an addiction.

My mother was a registered nurse, trapped in a miserable, abusive marriage with four children and no support system. Despite my mother's education and decent paying position, we lived a life filled with poverty. The majority of wealth she attained was forcibly taken by my father. This was a major funding source for Dad's drug usage.

It was usually around Mom's payday that the bruises would surface. There was one particular night that burns deep in my memory. It reminds me of just how cruel, manipulating and deceitful my father was. It was Mom's payday and there seemed to be a disagreement about Mom handing over money to my father.

In order to resolve this issue, my father decided to involve his four children in this decision making process. The dynamics among the children alone was an incredible sight. My oldest brother worshipped my father and really wanted to please him. I, on the other hand, did not worship my father. I was my mother's biggest ally and supporter. I did, though, have a fear of him. My youngest brother was the middle child and did not feel a part of anything and rarely said much of anything. My youngest sister was little and confused.

My father knew his children feared him and hoped this would work to his advantage. Dad decided to gather his children in their bedroom and sat us on the floor in a circle. He began by telling his children that he needed some money to take care of some important business and my mother didn't think he should have this money. My mother sat on the bed, where he sat as well, silently listening to his sermon. He went on to say, he would give her the money back but it was really important he have this money. My mother was frightened. Not because she expressed this verbally, but because her eyes revealed what she felt inside.

My father proposed a vote be taken as to whether or not Mom should supply his need for money. He wanted a show of hands from his children, who he claimed would be the deciding factor. Of course, we were all for being a part of this major decision. We had no real concept of what was going on. We just thought this was another type of game that we could be a part of. It made us feel really important.

I was probably the most sophisticated of the bunch and was not really feeling this moment. I, definitely, did not trust my father but I was not really sure what he was up to.

Dad asked the question, "How many of you think your mother should give me the money?" The hands did not go up at first. Everyone hesitated to raise their hand. We each looked at each other to see who would be bold enough to answer this question with a silent raising of the hand.

My oldest brother raised his hand, stating, "I think she should give him the money. He said he would give it back." My youngest brother half raised his hand. It was obvious he did not want to agree, but did not want to deal with Dad's potential anger either.

Dad, getting a real sense for this situation, changed the question. Stating, "Okay, let's try this. How many of you think your mother shouldn't give me the money?"

I immediately raised my hand, stating, "We need the money for food and bills. I agree with my mother." I could see Dad's anger at my response. I glared at my younger brother and sister and they agreed with their big sister. My older brother still stood by his position.

I immediately informed my father, "I guess you lost. It's three to one, so you don't get the money." Dad tipped his head back and glared at my mother. He was eerily silent for a moment. Then he surprisingly stated, "Your daughter is right. I lost the vote. It's three to one. Your mother gets to keep the money. I'm going to step out for a while. You guys get ready for bed."

Elated with the smoothness of this process we readied ourselves for bedtime. We felt relieved when Dad didn't seem to get upset. Mom kissed us good night and Dad left to do whatever he was going to do. Feeling Mom was safe, we weren't going to starve, and Dad had left without incident, we all slept soundly.

Come morning, we all got up with the same cheerfulness that we had retired with. That is, until we saw Mom. Mom was black and blue from head to toe. We all looked at her battered body and worse than that, her sad, weary face. I sent my younger siblings out of the room and asked my mother what happened.

Mom very quietly stated, "This is what happens when you disagree with your father." I didn't know what to say. I hurt so badly for my mother. I did not know how to comfort her. Besides, I don't think there was anything in the world that could have made her feel better. That picture of her, on that day, haunts me to this day. I vowed not to let anyone treat me this way.

My feelings for my father have always been complicated. He was my father and I knew I was supposed to love him. I still couldn't help feeling as long as he were breathing, we would be miserable. The majority of my young life was spent wishing he were dead. This desire came with incredible guilt, but my instincts told me that life would never be good as long as he had breath in his body.

My father was a complicated person. He was an extremely handsome man with an entertaining sort of personality. He was bronze in complexion, and had wavy, jet-black hair. He could have possibly been mistaken for Hispanic or Cuban. He had an incredible singing voice and could fluently speak six different languages. His conversations were intelligent in nature and he was a wonderful cook.

I found it so sad and unfortunate that Dad had wasted his life being controlled by the forces of addiction. It seemed to be such an incredible waste to watch my father never tap into his phenomenal potential.

In my youth, I could never understand why he couldn't just stop using drugs. I questioned whether or not he ever really loved us. If he did, he would stop hurting us; he would stop doing drugs, right? It wasn't until later on in my life that I would have some insight into why he was who he was. Back then, I had no comfort around his cruelty.

I witnessed many of society's greatest ills within my own family structure. My home was used as a shooting gallery for heroin addicts. When my mother was working, we were left in the care of my father. Days at home with Dad were usually spent isolated upstairs with strict orders not to come downstairs. For hours we would be upstairs bored, waiting for the time when we could finally come downstairs or go outside and play. As children we were curious in nature and would often sneak to the bottom of the stairs. We wanted to know what it was Dad and his friends were doing. As a result of my curiosity, I have witnessed junkies injecting themselves in places I didn't realize veins existed.

If we weren't upstairs, we would be sitting in a car somewhere. We would all be crammed into a car, waiting for hours for Dad to return. Four children locked inside a small car was not very comfortable. This was usually in a seedy part of town. Being so young, we had no idea of the purpose of this venture. What we did know is it would be a long time before Dad came back. Those hours in either an extremely hot car or a very cold car, cramped up together, were pure torture.

What was really frightening were times when Dad would be high as a kite, driving the car. There were several accidents as a result of Dad "nodding out" from the effects of the drug. I remember each trip, tapping Dad to alert him that the light had just changed to green and he needed to wake up. Thank God, none of us have ever been seriously injured.

All memories of my father were not horrendous. There was a part of him that warranted feelings of love. Although Dad was the source of abuse, I always felt a sense of safety when it came to potential harm from any outside sources. It was understood, he would never let anyone hurt us. His mentality was that we were his property and he could do what he wanted to do, but no one else could do anything bad to us.

Dad had unique ways of demonstrating his ability to provide for our needs. One particular incident stands out for me. Despite the abnormality of its nature; in our world this was normal behavior.

Mom had alerted Dad to the fact that we were in desperate need of shoes. Our shoes were tight, dirty, and full of holes. It was obvious something needed to be done. My mother gave my father money to purchase the shoes. My father took us on a

16

shopping spree for our shoes. We were extremely excited at the prospect of obtaining something brand spanking new and not something that was handed down from either a church, a family member or a thrift store.

As we entered the store, we immediately headed straight to the department that housed shoes. My father told us to look at the shoes and decide which pair we wanted. The price didn't matter. He was going to make sure we got the pair of shoes of our own individual choice. We each tried on the shoes of our liking. Dad ensured each pair fit properly. It was customary for Dad to have one of his friends accompany us to the store. This trip was no exception to this rule.

Dad instructed each of us to put our old pair of shoes on the shelf, replacing the new pair that we wanted. He further told us to put on our new pair of shoes. We did as we were told. As we were leaving the store, we noticed store employees began to quicken their pace. Every staff member seemed to be moving very fast in our direction. It became apparently clear we were being followed. We all hurriedly got into the car. We were fully aware of the fact that Dad had showed us how to steal our own shoes.

Once in the car, there were people chasing the car, yelling at my father and his friend to stop. Simultaneously, steaks and other products from the store were coming out of Dad and his friend's clothing. Our reaction to this predicament was strange. We found this endeavor to be hilarious. We stuck out our tongues at the people chasing us and stuck up our middle fingers. We thought this was the funniest thing and saw nothing wrong with this.

This was the beginning of our short career as shoplifters. It was guaranteed that every time we had gone shopping with anyone, we would all have a stash in the car under the seat.

Corporal punishment was the most utilized form of discipline during my childhood. Spankings were common. It has now become an area of great controversy. There is now a fine line between discipline and abuse.

My father, of course, took this to another level. Spanking isn't quite the definition of what we were subjected to. I think the word "beatings" better defines our discipline. Dad would beat us with belts, extension cords and his heavy hands. If he wasn't physically punishing us, we may have to stand in a corner for hours with one foot off of the floor. Of course, if you didn't want this form of punishment to turn into a beating you better keep your face to the wall and you definitely did not want your foot to touch the floor.

There was one punishment I will never forget. We were riding in the car after having picked up Mom from work. It was a common rule in our household that you better not tell Mom anything you witnessed Dad doing while she was at work. It was my tendency to update Mom on all the goings-on while she was away.

Mom had a twin sister and her husband was one of my father's partners in crime. He also was addicted to heroin. Earlier that day, my uncle had come over to the house with another woman. My uncle, his friend, and my father had been in the basement shooting up heroin and listening to records. Mom had found out about this and decided to confront my father. My father was furious that someone had the nerve to rat him out, especially after he warned us to keep our mouths shut.

I was immediately the target of my father's rage. Dad automatically assumed I had been the source of Mom's knowledge. I had not ratted him out. Not this time, anyway. He began yelling and cursing at me. I denied telling Mom anything. He obviously did not believe in my innocence in this matter. Dad decided he was going to teach me to keep my big mouth shut. At the first red light, he turned around in his seat, balled up his huge fist and sent it crashing into my mouth. My mouth began bleeding and my tooth was knocked out.

I cried for a brief moment and then the anger kicked in. I stop myself from crying and began to wipe my mouth with tissues Mom had provided. I refused to let him see me crying. I decided to glare at him with a look of pure hatred and disgust. I would not let him win by seeing the hurt and pain I had felt. I believe my reaction may have even shocked him a bit.

I soon recognized I had discovered a new skill. I had taught myself how to shut off emotions that were too overwhelming for me to handle and tap into feelings that were a little more comforting, like anger. Eventually, I took this technique to a new level. I learned not only how to shut off feelings of emotion, I could actually allow a feeling of numbness to take over.

Not only could I stop the tears, I also managed to shut down every emotion I had, including feelings of anger. This was the beginning of something I would use later on in my adult life to keep myself from going totally insane. For this, I thanked my father.

Not every aspect of my father's character was bad or negative. I suspect there is a level of goodness inside of everyone. I have some fond memories of my father. During my preadolescent years I was in and out of the hospital for a much needed spinal fusion. This is a surgical procedure used to correct severe cases of scoliosis or curvature of the spine. This is a very involved process which requires the insertion of a metal rod into the back. The rod is placed against the spinal column with a bone removed from the hip area. Hospitalization was necessary for specific intervals.

Initially, to correct this condition, I was fitted with a body cast. The cast is molded on your body as you lay on a device that stretches you. The machine is strapped underneath your chin and around your upper body. It is also strapped around your waist. The machine is then cranked by a handle that pulls the straps in the opposite direction. This is cranked until your body is as straight as it can possible get.

You are then left in this position as a cast made of plaster is formed around your body. This cast is fit from directly under your chin to just underneath your pelvis area. It was painful and difficult to lie in that position. The pain was excruciating and it took a long time.

My initial stay at the hospital was for an approximate two-week period of time. I remained flat on my back in this first body cast for two weeks prior to the actual surgery. This was a hospital for children and I hated being away from home. My father would come to the hospital everyday to visit with me. I hated the food at the hospital and would eat minimal amounts.

My father would cook a full meal for me daily and bring it to the hospital during lunch and sit with me while I ate. My dad did not look like other children's dads. He was always under the influence of some type of narcotic and his appearance was similar to that of a street person. Although embarrassed, I was grateful and happy to see my father.

After the surgery, I remember waking up to my family in the recovery room. I had lost a considerable amount of blood and required a blood transfusion. I was placed in another body cast during the surgical procedure and had to remain flat on my back. I could not walk in this cast. I was able to go home to a hospital bed that was awaiting my arrival in the middle of our living room. I remained in this position for close to two months.

During this time, all of my needs were tended to by my family members. My father made sure my care was a team effort. This included scratching areas that itched, to changing my bedpans.

Following this time period at home, I had to go back to the hospital and have my cast changed. I had to learn how to walk again in this newly created cast. It took several weeks before I could leave the hospital to reside at home. I was sent home for a three-month period of time.

I went back to the hospital to finally have this cast removed and once again had to learn how to walk without its weight. During each hospital stay, my father remained consistent.

There were other times when we would see my father quite vulnerable. He would sit us down as a family, talk about God and cry. He would talk about changing his life and made promises he never managed to keep.

I always dreamed Dad would change his ways. He was my only example of a male figure; good, bad and ugly. I thought all men were like Dad. The sins of my father became my lifelong persecution.

Chapter Three

Passive Strength

MY MOTHER AND FATHER were like night and day; salt and pepper. Even at a young age, I knew my mother was a strong person. My mother was sweet, naive, and far from street savvy. Despite the lack of material things that were evident in our home, my mother took advantage of everything she possibly could to keep her children involved in positive activities.

With very limited resources, Mom somehow found a way to keep us in Catholic school for many years. I attended Catholic school until I entered high school. Mom always kept some form of religion instilled in us. We went to church every Sunday, even if we had to walk. There were times we would attend Pentecostal church, just because there was a bus that would take us there and bring us back.

I never understood the rituals and routines of the church. I just knew what we did was important. I recognized God as something that somehow helped my mother survive her hard life. The awareness of God's ability to keep my mom from the darkness of insanity, gave me some sense of His importance and power. I knew I had to keep God in my life as well. The only religious thing I understood fully as a youngster was the Ten Commandments. My mother would talk to us about them often. I wanted to be a good person and live by His commandments. Hell was a scary notion and heaven sounded wonderful.

Although my desire to be a good girl was sincere, I couldn't always live up to this idea. I was a child who had to grow up fast and it was survival of the fittest. The neighborhoods in which I lived were no better than the surroundings in my immediate household. It was sometimes hard to discern what was bad versus what was normal. Where I came from, everyone had problems like my father.

Mom, on the other hand, tried her best to keep us surrounded by people who exemplified stability and were positive influences in our lives. She kept us involved in mentor programs, after school activities, camps, sporting events and any other affordable or free program she could enroll us into.

As a young, impressionable girl, I saw my mother as the epitome of perfection. She was beautiful and smart. She spent quality time with her children, despite all of the disorder in her life. My mother was a hard worker and was respected on her job. She kept the house spotless, despite our lack of materials things.

My mother didn't have much of a life. Her only interactions with adults were people she met at work and her twin sister, whom my father despised. Mom never went anywhere, ever, for social functions. One year, Dad decided he would allow Mom to go to a job Christmas party. I'm not sure if he had felt a bit of Christmas spirit or had just lost his mind.

Whatever his reasoning, this was a big event for her. I was excited to see my mother have an opportunity to get out and have some fun. At the same time, I wasn't too eager about being at home with Dad. Nevertheless, this was about Mom, not me.

Mom was nervous and excited at the same time. She wanted to get dressed as quickly as possible before anything could happen to stop her opportunity to socialize. Mom had finally gotten herself dressed and out the door. Things at home were quiet and there was nothing particular going on. We had been downstairs in the living room watching television with Dad when all of a sudden there was a loud knock on the door.

We weren't expecting anybody and were a little alarmed at the loudness of the knock. The knock turned into banging. Several voices were yelling, "Open up. It's the police." Quick as lightning, Dad shut off the television and all of the lights. He instructed his children to duck down in the living room and not to open the door.

Dad ran upstairs and began flushing drugs into the toilet. He was hiding upstairs yelling, "Don't let them in. Hold them off." I remember being very frightened as the police were now trying to break down the doors and were shining flashlights into the house.

We had all been pushing our weight against the front door so the police officers couldn't get in. The officers stopped working on the front door and had gone around to the back door. They managed to break into this door and were immediately attacked by my brothers and the dog.

The police officers were very angry that these two little kids had tried to beat them up. My father, hiding upstairs, did not help to calm their anger. Quite the contrary, this made them even more upset. What kind of man would allow his children to deal with this situation while he hid upstairs? They snatched my father from upstairs, handcuffed him, and put him into the police car.

They wanted to know where my mother was. I told them she had gone to a job Christmas party less than an hour ago. Next thing you know, I'm having Mom paged at the Christmas party because there is an emergency at home. Poor Mom. She never got a break. She never got a break from Dad either. After all that drama, he was out of jail and home the next day.

24

Mom was so caged in her marriage. Dad wouldn't allow her the opportunity to attend her own father's funeral. She could barely mourn his death. I remember seeing her, standing by the kitchen stove, very upset. She was unusually quiet and had tears welling up in her eyes. I asked my father what was wrong with Mom. He very casually stated, "Leave your mother alone. Grandpa died and she's upset."

I knew my mother had to be devastated. She adored her father. Yet, she stood there, at the stove, cooking and cleaning just like every other day of her life. She wasn't even given a moment to grieve. She had to tend to her family like any other day. Dad did not pitch in to help her. Instead, he just lay down on the couch and watched her as she paid attention to his every need and whim. I tried to comfort my mother. I instructed my siblings to be on their best behavior today. That was the only way I could think of helping to console Mom.

In my heart, I knew Mom would never forgive Dad for this. If she did find forgiveness, she would definitely never forget. This had to be worse than any beating or cruelty Dad had ever inflicted on Mom. Despite her grief, Mom just kept going. She found her solace in her children. She tried to be the best mother she could possibly be.

Mom utilized whatever tools she had. She constantly instilled in her children as many values and morals as she could. She never led us to believe Dad was doing the right thing. She didn't bash my father either. But she did teach us right from wrong.

Mom wasn't much in the way of a disciplinarian. When she tried to give us spankings, she never ever spanked us enough to make us cry. As a matter of fact, she would give us a so-called spanking and we would put on a stage play and pretend we were crying from sheer pain. Later on, we would go in our bedroom and crack up with laughter. Mom, on the other hand, would have tears in her eyes from thinking she hurt her babies.

We kept this act going, mainly because we didn't want Dad to find out, so that he could inflict the punishment.

I also learned that my mother was creative in dealing with my father. When things got really bad and Mom needed a break from his bullying and violence, she had devised a plan that surprisingly worked to keep him away from her.

My father would tell us that Mom was crazy. You see, Mom's family was from the Caribbean islands. Mom had told Dad that she had taken some of his hair from a brush and put it in a jar filled with urine. She told him if he didn't stop bothering her she would put a curse on him. She let him know this was practiced on the islands when people wanted revenge on someone who had done them wrong.

I marveled at the fact that it kept my father still. He honestly believed Mom could put an old island curse on him. Of course, we knew she made it up. All that mattered was that he believed it and it would usually work.

Mom had her hands full with four children and a crazy husband. As kids we were pretty bad. Our environment definitely affected our outcome. Despite this, Mom did her best to maintain her family and consistently teach her kids decent ways of living.

I never saw her as a weak person. I admired her incredible strength. Her strength didn't look like strength to outsiders looking in. To others, she may have even appeared to be passive, allowing herself to remain a victim, never fighting back. I recognized her surface passivity was her strength. It kept her alive and able to care for her children. At even a young age, I recognized her survivor skills.

Fortunately, she had the wisdom and insight to realize that I would need some extra tools to work with later on. Keeping her children in the church, teaching us right from wrong (despite our environment), spending quality time with her children, and those incredibly boring lectures she would give us, would all pay off one day. I did not want the same type of life she had when I became an adult. Little did I know, I would become every bit of my mother.

Chapter Four

Trickle Down Effect

AS AN ADOLESCENT, THE neediness, the desire to be loved was massive. I was willing to accept anything in my life. Besides, I knew no other way. I had no concept of what a healthy relationship was supposed to look like. The only relationships I witnessed were those flooded with violence. My parents' relationship set the tone for what I perceived to be a healthy lifestyle. The irony lay in the thoughts I had growing up that I would never be in a situation like my mother was. Somehow, I believed I would come out of this situation smarter and wiser.

I was totally oblivious to the fact that I had not been exposed to what a non-dysfunctional, solid relationship looked like. The only thing I could base my thoughts on were the fact that I knew, in my gut, there was something wrong with what I was exposed to. None of the families on television were like my parents' marriage. I yearned for that type of happiness. I wanted the *Leave It To Beaver* life. Of course, we don't always get what we want.

My first love was a big disappointment for me. I was 15 years of age and had no self-esteem. Life at home was different now. Dad was incarcerated in a maximum security prison in

New York State. The penal system had finally caught up to him. He had been serving time for an armed robbery conviction. He had one prior felony conviction and was now serving a five-year sentence for his latest conviction.

As a teenager, I was very skinny and very shy; painfully shy. I didn't fit in anywhere. My complexion is very light, despite the fact that both of my parents are African-American. Individuals of my own ethnicity didn't really take to me because it was their feeling that I thought I was better somehow because my skin was light and my hair was fairly straight. Individuals of Caucasian descent knew I was different than they were and they weren't willing to accept me either. This was extremely confusing for me as I couldn't see myself as different from any other African-American. This added to my lack of self-esteem and value as a person.

I found myself attracted to a young man, who seemed to be smart, sophisticated and had the potential to be a success in life. He was book smart, popular, worked, drove a car and there were several girls who wanted to be his girlfriend. There was one problem. He already had a girlfriend.

Although I felt some moral conviction about being attracted to somebody else's boyfriend, I just could not seem to help myself and the way I felt. I wanted him to notice me. I felt so insignificant as a person at that time, that the least amount of attention would have fed into my hunger for what I thought to be love. Eventually, he did pay attention to me. I was so enamored with this young man, that I threw all sense of morality out of the window. I believed he loved me. It became meaningless that he was cheating on his girlfriend. I never thought about her feelings, only my own need to be desired, to be loved.

I remember the day he took my virginity. This had been an event that I did not want so much for myself. I did not even look forward to it. This was the beginning of my pattern of being a people pleaser. I had constantly made excuses or thought of ways to get out of this predicament I had seemingly gotten myself into. The day came, when I gave of myself in the most intimate, private way. What I felt on that day currently haunts me and has never left my memory. Twenty-six years later, I remember the date of this event and at each anniversary date, I feel a sense of sadness.

I imagined this would be some incredibly romantic moment that would live in my memory forever. Instead, I remember feeling cheap, used, and a bad person. I cried afterwards for hours, alone. I knew I had made a terrible mistake. I knew it was the beginning of a life of many disappointments. My dream of him leaving his girlfriend to be with me, never took place. It added to my lack of self-worth.

Getting beyond this rejection was a tremendously painful part of my journey through adolescence. I cried, I moaned, I wailed. I prayed and prayed for this pain to stop and for God to please bring him back to me.

I knew that God was the answer but never fully knew what that was supposed to mean. I didn't read the Bible and when I did, I did not understand what I was reading. I searched through the Bible for comfort. It did not work. The only chapter of the Bible that I could read and understand was the book of Proverbs. I would read Proverbs over and over to help make sense of this huge amount of pain I struggled with.

I've heard it said that time heals all wounds. In my case, time wasn't a factor. I needed an immediate answer, a Band-Aid, to stop the wound from bleeding; to cover up the anguish.

It was the last year of high school and I was the same broken person. I met Daniel at this time. He was not someone I had an interest in. As a matter of fact, he was downright annoying. He was significantly shorter than I was and a total pest.

Daniel was very persistent. He finally broke me down. He managed to get me to agree to go out with him on a date. The first time I went out with him was strange. I remember him introducing me to someone else. I couldn't connect the importance of this meeting. Following this date, he would constantly ask me what I thought of his friend.

I informed him I was absolutely not interested in his friend. I went a step further and made him aware of the fact that I was barely interested in him. Time went on and I guess Daniel kind of grew on me. Daniel began to introduce me to many of his friends and family. His family, I believe, is what kept me linked and interested in him.

Spending time with his family, made my family look like foreigners. I wanted that type of family and was happy to be welcomed by them. Daniel was aware of my upbringing and where I came from. He knew I wanted to be on my own. He told me his sister, Andrea, had her own apartment and was looking for a roommate.

Andrea and I were in the same homeroom and were already friendly. I became interested in viewing the apartment. She had been living in an in-law apartment that was situated on the top floor of a home owned by her older sister, Marcy, and her brother-in-law, Jason. Daniel wanted me to meet them as well.

As we drove up to the home, I was amazed at how beautiful it was. I had not been exposed to this type of environment. My family and I had lived in housing projects. The idea of owning a home was just that; an idea, a notion, a dream. My home was a source of embarrassment for me. I did not want my friends to see how we were living. We never had decent furniture and my siblings and I slept on mattresses on the floor.

Mom always taught me to keep my surroundings clean. She made sure our lack of material things did not affect its presentation. This value became an ingrained element of my character. If I had one piece of furniture, it was the cleanest piece of furniture you had ever seen. It was the material wealth that I admired.

My father, a smoker, nodding out from the heroin, often fell asleep on the couch with a cigarette in either his hand or mouth. There was an incident where he actually set the couch on fire as he was lying on it. Our couch was always ruined by cigarette holes.

Walking into this home was like a dream to me. I definitely wanted to live here. I was introduced to Marcy, and her one-year-old child. Her husband had not come home yet. While waiting to meet him, I was taken to the upstairs apartment I may be sharing with Andrea.

It was a wonderful apartment. I hoped this would work out. This visit seemed to be going well. Marcy and I seemed to get along very well. After sometime, her husband came home. When he walked in the door, my jaw almost fell to the floor.

I recognized him and he recognized me. This is the guy Daniel tried to set me up with. What kind of lowlife was he? How could he possibly try to set me up with his sister's husband? I kept my cool and never said a word to Marcy. I could not get out of their home fast enough.

Once outside of the home, I wanted answers. Daniel really didn't give me any. He just said it wasn't his brother-in-law that I had previously met. It was someone who looked like him.

It wasn't long before I moved into the apartment. Andrea was rarely home, and I was basically left alone. I would often spend time with Marcy downstairs and we became close friends. Two weeks later, Andrea moved out and Daniel moved in. Eventually, I graduated from high school. I barely made it. That last year of high school was difficult for me. Not because I couldn't do the work, but because emotionally I was a wreck and could not focus on my schoolwork.

Initially, moving into this apartment with Daniel was a thrilling experience for me. We shopped together and brought new furniture and decorations for the apartment. There was no television. We could not really afford it. If I wanted to watch television, I would have to wait to go downstairs and watch it with Marcy.

It wasn't long before Daniel's true character revealed itself. On average, I was left alone and kept isolated from everyone. I would sit in the apartment for hours with no telephone, no television, no radio, no nothing. I became an avid reader during this time. I enjoyed reading and found myself reading anything I could get my hands on.

The only door to the apartment had a deadbolt lock on it that could only be unlocked from the outside. Daniel would lock me into the apartment and take off. The only interactions I had were with Marcy and her family members downstairs. I was totally isolated from my family. The only time I would see Mom was on Sunday. I would go to her house once a week to do laundry. On the minimal occasions when Daniel came home, we usually fought. There were many fights between us. The two of us would scrap like two men fighting in a bar.

Holidays were spent alone, locked up in an apartment. He would be gone for days at a time. When he decided it was time to come home, he would usually have marks on his neck indicating he had been having a good time with some other woman. The only reason I remained in that situation was my desire to appear to be anything other than a failure in this relationship. I was also mesmerized by the huge diamond ring he had given me. I was his fiancée! Someone actually wanted to marry me. I felt honored.

The violence between Daniel and myself was increasingly getting worse. Mom came to the apartment one day and could clearly see I was unhappy. The expression on my face revealed all of the pain, loneliness and sadness inside. Mom told me the door to her home was open and if I ever wanted to come back I could. Mom's next declaration felt magical at the time. She told me, "You don't have to live the way I've lived. Don't make the same mistakes I did. You can always come back home." This sounded wonderful. Anything was better than living like this. My father was still incarcerated which made this prospect even more desirable.

I began to plan my getaway. I had made arrangements for a moving truck. I packed my belongings for their delivery to my mother's house. I patiently waited for my escape. The day finally came. It was a day like no other. While Daniel was at work, my brothers came and moved me out of the apartment and into Mom's house. This was all done before he got home from work. Marcy and her husband had been gone as well. No one knew I was leaving. Knowing Daniel would be coming home to an empty apartment was a huge source of enjoyment and pleasure for me.

As anticipated, the phone call came wondering what was going on. I let him know I was totally miserable and would be staying with my family. He did not like this one bit, but knew there was nothing he could do about it. It was shortly afterwards, that I discovered I was pregnant. I was only 18 years of age and hadn't a clue as to what I was doing.

My relationship with Daniel continued and we remained engaged during most of my pregnancy. I believe he stuck around because his family insisted on it. Daniel always expressed prejudice feelings toward African-Americans and often referred to my people using the "N" word. I found this highly offensive. He was of Puerto Rican descent and felt he was somehow better.

In light of this, I don't think Daniel was thrilled about the prospects of having a half-black child. As a matter of fact, he often said he hoped his child didn't have nappy hair, a big nose, and big lips. He and I really did not get along. He made me sick to my stomach. I felt forever linked to this idiot because we were having a child together.

In my seventh month of pregnancy, he and I were going to visit his parents. Just before we entered the house, an argument ensued. We were standing on an ice-covered porch. Our argument began to heat up and he pushed me. I slipped and fell, landing on my swollen belly. Luckily, there was no damage done to myself or to the baby. As a result of this incident, we realized our being together was not a good thing to do. The engagement was off.

We parted ways and he quickly found himself another girlfriend. It was very painful to see him with another woman especially while I was carrying his child. He could have at least waited until the baby was born. But, he was incredibly selfish and cared only about his needs.

My mother was a big source of support during the remainder of my pregnancy. The day I went into labor, Daniel came to the hospital. It was difficult for me to have to endure him throughout this very emotional process. To my surprise, he was very supportive and kind throughout our daughter's birth.

During the course of my labor, the strangest thing happened. My labor was slow and I was moved into another room. In the bed next to me was a woman who had just given birth. We were separated by a curtain. The nursing staff had just entered the room and were trying to communicate with this woman. She did not speak English.

They needed an interpreter and decided they would ask Daniel to help them out. He was more than willing to help until he discovered what it is they wanted him to communicate to her. Apparently, the woman had delivered twins shortly before. One of her babies did not survive. They needed to tell this woman that she had just lost one of her babies. Not only that, they wanted Daniel to tell her this.

Here I am, barely 19 years of age, and scared to death. The woman next to me just lost her child. I was afraid of what could happen to me and my baby. What if my child were born dead?

Daniel asked me if I would be okay with him helping out this woman. I just wanted the pain to stop and couldn't concern myself with anything else. I instructed him to do what he felt he needed to do.

I could hear Daniel behind the curtain, speaking in Spanish. There was a slight pause and I heard a series of sniffles. Then the woman started crying an awful cry. It was so piercing, so gut wrenching, that I began to cry for her. After approximately 20 minutes of listening to her uncontrollable sobbing, she attempted to absorb the shocking news of her newborn child's death. Once the situation had calmed down somewhat, the nursing staff decided to come into the room again.

They weren't coming to check on me though. They wanted another favor from Daniel. They requested he ask the woman if she desired the opportunity to see her baby, her dead baby. As a grieving mother, it was no great shock to learn she wanted to see her child. She needed to say goodbye. Without hesitation, they wheeled this dead baby into the room, right next to me, for all to see. I watched as she held her baby, sobbed heavily and rocked back and forth singing softly.

All kinds of thoughts were going through my head. I imagined my own child being born dead. This made for a hard, hard labor. Thank God, my child was born, complication free. She was healthy and beautiful. I named her Monique. My new journey into motherhood had just begun.

It wasn't long after her birth that Daniel revealed his intentions towards fatherhood. His family, on the other hand, absolutely loved her and spent a lot of time spoiling her. I would bring my daughter to his mother's home, where he was living at the time, for weekend visitation. If it weren't for their interest in seeing her and spending time with her, he would have never been involved.

There were times when I would have to resort to begging him for money, just to buy diapers or get the things she needed. I was receiving public assistance then and had a limited income. His family did all that they could, but it wasn't their responsibility. Eventually, I obtained a court order for child support. Monique never learned Daniel was her father until she was approaching her fourth birthday. He would attend functions and events with his family members but rarely interacted with her during these occurrences. I had heard, through the grapevine, Daniel was denying Monique was his daughter. I was told he made nasty remarks about not having a "nigger" for a daughter. I never knew if this was true, but it hurt just the same.

Contrarily, Monique's appearance did not fit into Daniel's perception of what African-American people looked like. Her hair was straight and she had small features. She was usually perceived as a person of Hispanic heritage. Despite her outward appearance, Monique has never identified herself as Hispanic. She never acknowledged that part of her culture; despite my attempts to expose her to all parts of herself. I never spoke ill of her father. I never wanted her to feel any parts of her were bad or negative. This is something I learned from my mother.

As an adult, his lack of involvement in her life remains an open wound. I hope one day she sees it as a loss for him and not for herself. She is a beautiful person that he has never had the pleasure of knowing. I can recognize the blessing created out of this disappointment in my life. For that reason alone, I would never regret having Daniel in my life.

As I journeyed into my new role as a single parent, I felt incredibly guilty and ashamed. Becoming a young, unmarried parent was not what I had dreamed of for my life. I had resigned myself to believe I wasn't entitled to a better life. Life outside of the ghetto was difficult to envision. I yearned for more. I wanted better. It just didn't appear to be a realistic goal for me.

I felt like a failure and a disappointment. I wanted a complete family. I made up my mind. She deserved a father and I deserved a husband. I was on a mission to find a father for my child. I knew this was a goal I could attain. What I failed to consider was at what cost would I attain this goal?

Chapter Five

They Say You Marry Your Father

IT WAS SHORTLY AFTER my disappointing relationship with Daniel that I met Jose. Monique was approximately seven months in age and fatherless. I, similar to my mother, wanted desperately to have a father for my child. I felt, once again, unworthy of love. Condemnation also played a major role in what I was experiencing emotionally. It seemed logical that my daughter was without a father because there was something wrong with me that caused everyone I loved to walk away and abandon me. Along with feelings of self-blame came enormous humiliation and shame. My religious upbringing left me with extreme conviction about being so young and a mother with no husband. Daniel's obvious lack of interest in his daughter really was a twist of the knife in an already open wound.

Jose was pleasing to the eye. He was bronze in completion and had jet-black, wavy hair. He was a pure charmer. There was an exciting edge to him that hooked me into him quickly. I felt much gratitude to have such a handsome guy interested in me.

I was far removed from appreciating God's gifts to me and my own worthiness as a person. I thought I was the lucky one to have him in my life. Jose was instantly attached to my daughter. He was wonderful with her and just as thrilled, as I was when she reached a milestone or did something cute. Still reeling from Daniel's rejection of her, I was addicted to this relationship fast.

The abuse started early on. The first incident happened less than a month after we had started dating. Jose and I decided to take a walk to the nearby store. It was a snowy evening and my parents did not mind watching my daughter while we took our brief walk. The walk to the store happened without incident. It was during the course of our travels back from the store that took a strange turn.

Jose and I decided it was time for some fun. The snowball fight began. It was silly, fun, and full of laughter. It soon became something much more sinister. The snowballs were flying and the laughter was rich; that is, until the unthinkable happened. I got lucky and landed a snowball square into the center of Jose's chest. All of a sudden the laughter stopped. I heard a slight groan coming from his direction and noticed he had been slightly doubled over for a quick second.

I immediately expressed great concern and apologized for being such a good target. Like a quick flash of lightning, I felt a hard fist hit me square in the eye, knocking me backwards into a nearby set of bushes. I was totally stunned. Realizing what he had done, he immediately helped me out of the bushes, expressing great remorse for what he had just done.

He informed me that my eye looked very bad. He began to put packs of snow on it to stop the apparent swelling. I actually wasn't concerned about my eye or my safety with this hot-tempered man. I was much more worried about how I was going to explain my black eye to my parents, especially my father.

Astonishingly, Jose volunteered to go back to the house with me and explain to my parents what he had just done. He wanted to tell the truth! Was he crazy? My father would kill him.

Worse than that, they would quickly put an end to this relationship before it got started. I definitely did not want that.

I was flooded with a variety of thoughts and emotions. I knew what happened was a bad thing. Logically, my mind informed me of this. But my desire to be wanted and loved outweighed any sense of logic. Instead, I was worried about who was going to make me feel special. Who would be willing to spend time with me and another man's child? Who was going to care about my daughter? Certainly not her biological father. I was overwhelmed with the fear of being alone as well as being saddled with the guilt and shame of being a young, single parent.

I couldn't allow my parents to take away my crutch. Besides, this was my business, right? Who are they to say anything to me? Jose didn't really mean to hit me. He just reacted to my mistake. It was my fault. Maybe I played just a little too rough. He apologized and said it would never happen again. I believed him. I had successfully justified what had happened in my mind. My focus wasn't on what had just occurred. I shifted my focus and created a credible lie to cover up the abuse I had just endured.

When Jose and I walked through the door, my parents took one look at me, then at him. They demanded an explanation for what they were seeing. I started talking right away. I had concocted a story about a snowball fight that got out of hand. I told my parents I had been hit in the eye with a snowball by mistake.

My mother knew firsthand what abuse looked like. My father knew it better than she did. Neither one of them fully accepted this story. My father sternly informed Jose that he better not ever put his hands on his daughter. Jose poured on the charm and promised my father he would never do anything to hurt his daughter.

Not fully aware of the fact that I had just given Jose

41

permission to abuse me physically, I was thrilled that my parents (with reservation) were not going to terminate this relationship. I had just revealed to Jose that I was vulnerable and desperate enough to allow him to abuse me. Hence, the cycle of abuse had just begun.

Six months later, Jose and I were married. The first year of our marriage was a lonely time for me. Jose had enrolled into the Coast Guard and was stationed in Maryland. Monique and I waited several months before moving to Maryland from Massachusetts. We lived in military housing during this time period. Our apartment was big and the complex in which we lived had a huge swimming pool and tennis courts. Our apartment was sparsely furnished but kept spotlessly clean. We always had plenty of food.

I quickly became bored. I was far away from family and was not working or attending school or anything. During this time period, there was no abuse inflicted on me by Jose. Things ran pretty smoothly and I was miserable. Our marriage was ideal for Jose. Everything was focused around him and his needs. He and Monique were everything. I felt lonely. I had no friends or family around me. I was totally available for his each and every whim. I wanted to be back home. I was accustomed to working. In Massachusetts, I had family supports, I had a church home, and I had some friends to talk to.

The majority of my time was spent in the apartment with Monique, entertaining her. Jose was always away on a ship for extended periods of time. Occasionally, I would venture outside with Monique to the playground or the pool. I would engage in brief, casual conversations with other families that lived in the complex. I discovered a small church, not far from the apartment, that Monique and I would attend on Sunday. I never felt comfortable there. My only outlet was to call and write home as often as I could.

Summer had come around again and my younger sister, TC,

came to stay with me just before going back to school. I loved her company and dreaded her eventual departure. I missed home. I felt unproductive and unchallenged and wanted to be doing something with myself. TC had informed me that Dad was still up to no good. This bothered me greatly and I felt compelled to be with Mom to protect her from Dad.

I have an older half sister, Scherrie, that I had always been very close to. I had lost contact with her for a ten-year period and often thought about her. I have fond memories of her visits to Massachusetts during the summer months to spend time with her siblings and her father. My mother, although she was not her child, never treated Scherrie any different than her own biological children. Somehow, Scherrie had located my parents and made plans to visit them. She was an adult now with a family of her own. Scherrie was living in North Carolina at that time. Her plan was to stop in Maryland following her visit with my parents.

I eagerly anticipated my visit with Scherrie. Over the years, I had wondered where she was and missed her tremendously. True to her word, Scherrie stopped through to see my younger sister and I and meet her niece and brother-in-law. My older brother, Ricky, was also in the Coast Guard. Ricky, now married, was also living in Maryland. Seeing Scherrie was wonderful. We immediately connected. She expressed great worry and concern for my mom. Scherrie told me Dad was still stealing from Mom and continued to use drugs. While visiting Mom and Dad, Scherrie had gotten into an argument with Dad. She had gotten upset because her infant daughter had found a hypodermic needle on the floor.

Distressed at hearing this news, and feeling driven to protect my mother, I decided to pack my things and move back home. It didn't make sense to stay in Maryland. Jose was never home and my family needed me. My plan wasn't to stay away from my new husband for very long. But, just long enough to help take care of my mother and little sister.

I loaded my belongings into a small trailer hitched to the back of our car. Jose drove myself, Monique and TC to Massachusetts. He didn't appear to be upset that I was leaving. He promised to travel back and forth until I decided to come back.

Once back home, initially things were tolerable. That is, until Dad had stolen TC's sewing machine and pawned it. She was heartbroken. She cherished her sewing machine. As a result of his selfish actions, Dad and I became involved in a major argument. TC decided she was fed up with Dad and moved out of the house. Then, I discovered he had been stealing checks out of Mom's checkbook and was writing out checks to himself. He had the audacity to try this endeavor with my checkbook. That became the final straw that broke this camel's back.

Mom was tired of living this life and Dad's bullying ways. She saw no way out of this mess. I presented Mom with a proposal. I told Mom she could come back to Maryland with Monique and I. I still had an apartment there and there was plenty of room. She had reservations but entertained the idea.

Well, the confrontation between my father and I had finally happened. I let Dad know I was sick and tired of his drug habit and the way he treated my mother. I told him in no uncertain terms would I allow him to continue with his abusive ways. My father let me know he would do what he wanted to do and that my mother was his business and not mine. This heated exchange of words escalated. My father, in a rage, grabbed my mother by the neck and slammed her into the wall. Her feet were dangling off of the floor and he had no reservations about choking her. He had slammed her so hard that the wall caved in.

I grabbed the telephone and started to call the police. I let him know he would be arrested and that he better leave her alone right now. He dropped her and lunged at me with a knife. Although I put on a brave front, I wanted to wet my pants. I was so frightened!!! I kept my fear a secret. I acted as brave as I possibly could and instructed my mother to run out of the house with my daughter to the car. I notified everyone that the police were on the way. I decided I was going to present my father with an alternative. I told him to either get out of the way or cut me now. I further let him know that my mother was leaving with me.

He, with the knife in his hand, pointing at me, looked totally confused. I could see he was backed into a corner and did not know what to do. He dropped the knife. I ran out of the door with Monique and my mother. We ran down four flights of stairs, with as many pieces of clothing we could carry, baby in tow. It was at this time that the police arrived on the scene.

We followed the officers back into the house and grabbed more articles of clothing. The police gave my father the standard lecture and threatened to lock him up if he persisted in this type of behavior. Watching this, we knew we had better get out of town as quickly as possible. Functioning on pure adrenaline, we got into the car and just drove. Two hours later, we became weary and decided to stop at my aunt's home in New York. We decided to stay there for a while. This gave my mother a chance to think about what was going to happen next.

After a week or so, I was now ready to get on the road and get planted in Maryland. Mom made a major announcement. She strongly declared she was no longer going to run from this situation. She was going back to Massachusetts and her job. I questioned her sense of reality wondering how she would do this with Dad still in the home. She said she was tired of running and tired of the abuse. A plan was devised. I would assist Mom in obtaining a restraining order and have the police remove him from the home.

I can still visualize the seething fury on Dad's face as the police officers escorted him out of the home. It was many a sleepless nights before we realized Dad had resigned himself to respect the restraining order and leave us alone. His acceptance of the restraining order existed only as a result of the potential 20-year-prison sentence he faced if he violated parole.

Initially, he occupied a room in a boarding house. Eventually, he secured his own apartment in another part of town. He and I maintained a love/hate relationship. I was the target of Dad's blame for the situation that existed between he and my mother. Despite his disdain for me, I was the instrument he utilized to connect with Mom.

After a few months had passed, Dad came to the house, under my supervision, to visit with Mom. He begged and pleaded he be allowed to visit, stating he just wanted to talk to Mom. After all, she was still his wife. Mom agreed to talk to him as long as I was in the home as well. Dad came over that day and was very pleasant. He played with Monique for a while. She eventually fell asleep and was put down for a nap.

Dad and Mom began to have conversation and it appeared civil and peaceful. The conversation centered around their children and what was going on with each of them. It was at this point the telephone rang. I ran to answer it. I was anticipating a call from Jose, whom I missed a great deal. Sure enough, it was Jose on the telephone.

As I engaged in my telephone conversation, I simultaneously tried to pay attention to Mom and Dad. Their interactions remained polite and I quickly became engrossed in my telephone conversation. Dad, picking up on this, took full advantage of this situation.

Just before I hung up the telephone, I realized things had become strangely quiet. I told Jose I had to hang up the telephone because something was not right. I hung up the telephone as fast as I could and began to call out Mom's name. No answer. I searched the apartment for her whereabouts. I looked in each and every room and started to feel a sense of panic. Suddenly, I could detect muffled sounds coming out of the bathroom.

I ran to the outside door of the bathroom and asked Mom if she was in there. I heard a slight muffle and began banging on the door. I loudly exclaimed, "Open the door before I call the police." There was shuffling inside of the bathroom and what sounded like another muffled sound. This was clearly an attempted scream kept silent.

I threw my small body into the door with all my might. I urgently tried to get my mother out of there. I heard tussling with the lock on the door. The door had opened slightly. I peered inside of the bathroom and I noticed Mom. She was frightened and pressed firmly against the wall. My father immediately zipped up his pants. He flew out of the bathroom and ran out of the house. I helped Mom collect herself and checked to ensure she was without harm.

I asked Mom what had happened. I discovered Dad had forced her into the bathroom, held a knife to her throat, and attempted to rape her. Fortunately, he had not been successful. My disruption of his evil plot came in the nick of time.

As a derivative of this incident, assault charges were filed against my father. In the court proceeding, the focus became Mom's explanation for allowing my father back in the house since she had the restraining order. It was hard for the court system or anyone else for that matter to fully understand the dynamics involved in domestic violence situations. It was their feeling that the restraining order should have ended it. Little did they know, that when you are fearful of someone, you do whatever you have to do to keep the abuser from losing it. The lethality of the perpetrator is always at its peak when the victim leaves the relationship. Sometimes you have to appease that person to keep them from taking your life. Domestic violence itself can be a life sentence.

Another court date was set. The case wouldn't be heard for another three months. During this time period, my father took it upon himself to pester, threaten, plead, cry and demand she not go through with this. He had the audacity to enlist the services of members of the Black Muslim faith. They came to plead with my mother to take my father back. This was another way for Dad to attempt to play on Mom's goodness and faith. They insisted this was the Christian thing to do. My mother, with her newfound strength, informed them that if they were so concerned about doing the Christian thing, then they could take him and keep him.

You see, Dad had already been convicted of two felonies. The law had changed to a "three strikes and you're out" policy. Meaning, Dad would be sent away for a long, long time if he incurred a third felony.

Dad knew my mother was a kind, loving person with a soft heart. He saw this as a weakness and tried to tap into this for his own benefit. He was beginning to learn he had underestimated her strength. I knew she had to be a strong person to have tolerated him for so long.

When the case finally came back to court, Dad had been ordered to stay away from the home permanently. It was determined he could no longer come to the house for anything.

As an alternative, I would bring Monique to Dad's apartment for visits. Once a week, I helped him run errands and clean his apartment. My relationship with Dad was a strange one. We were both angry with each other. We constantly bickered. He often expressed how he felt I ruined his marriage and consistently blamed me for his separation from Mom. I was mad at him for everything he had put us through and simply because he had the nerve to be angry with me. Arguments were a common ritual. Regardless of this annoyance, I stayed faithful to helping him and maintaining his bond with Monique.

I received a telephone call from Dad one day. He told me he

had not been feeling well. He requested I take him to see a doctor due to problems he was experiencing with his leg that he had previously injured. While living in the boarding house, Dad had gotten into a fight with a former roommate which resulted in a fracture to his ankle.

Dad received medical instructions to wear a cast on this leg to promote proper healing. His ankle got progressively worse. He refused to follow the doctor's order. He was given further instruction not to walk on the ankle until it had completely healed. My father was determined to do what he wanted to do. He had a tendency to be stubborn, especially as it related to medical issues.

As a result of his stubbornness, his ankle never healed properly. Finally, a pin had to be surgically inserted into his ankle. By this time, it was pretty late in the game. An infection had spread in the bone and was wreaking havoc in his body.

I went to Dad's apartment to transport him to the doctor. When I saw him, I gasped at his appearance. He had lost a significant amount of weight. His cheeks were sunken into his face and his leg looked to be three times its normal size. I secured a wheelchair for him to keep the pressure off of his leg. I took him to the doctor's office as planned. He insisted I leave him there to handle this. His headstrongness revealed itself again and he insisted he would be fine. As usual we argued about this. This argument led to a discussion about everything he felt I had done to him.

I was sick and tired of this mess with him. I did as he said. I left him there. I didn't call him. I was tired of arguing with him all the time. I needed a break. I decided to allow some time to pass before contacting him.

One day TC and I had gone to the Laundromat to wash clothes. It was her birthday and a rather pleasant day. We were the only two left at home living with Mom. Ricky was still stationed in Maryland in the Coast Guard and my brother,

Chris, was struggling to find an adequate job and a decent place to live in the Virgin Islands.

My mother had planned a trip to the Virgin Islands to help get my brother back home. Her biggest goal was to visit her father's grave in St. Croix and finally say the goodbye she was never able to say. This was extremely important to her.

As TC and I arrived back home from washing clothes, Mom stood at the door watching us unload clothing from the car. As we approached the entranceway, we noticed her facial expression indicated something bad had happened. Mom began to tell us that she had received a telephone call from someone who knew my father. The caller told Mom that Dad had been in the hospital for almost two weeks in a coma.

We immediately went to the hospital to get an assessment of my father's situation. At the hospital, it was clear that my father was not doing well at all. He looked frightened and would sporadically slip in and out of consciousness. He was glad to see family at his bedside.

The hospital staff were pretty forthright about his condition. We were told that he had an infection in his leg that was spreading throughout his body. His veins had been severely impaired as a result of his intravenous drug usage. This presented a hardship for the medical staff as they diligently worked to create healing within his body. He required immediate surgery to attempt salvation of his leg. We were told his leg may have to be amputated. Amputation did not guarantee his survival. The infection was significant and was rapidly spreading throughout his body. Antibiotics were utilized first to determine whether or not the infection could be disseminated.

Mom was outwardly distraught. Her emotions were mixed. She struggled with taking her trip to the Virgin Islands versus leaving TC and I alone to handle this situation. Her decision was a tough one to make. Someone had to be available to make decisions regarding my father's treatment.

TC and I decided it was best to let my mother go, guilt free, to say goodbye to her father. We assured her we could handle the situation. Besides, she needed to bring my brother back home in case the worse happened to Dad. Ricky had been notified of Dad's condition and was traveling back to Massachusetts.

With reluctance, Mom left for the islands and TC and I were managing things as best we could. Ricky traveled back and forth from Maryland as much as the Coast Guard would permit. Dad's condition began to get worse. The medications were not working and a determination was made to entertain surgery. His leg had become gangrenous and there was a great possibility it would have to be amputated.

TC and I visited with Dad every day. Dad could not speak but he tried to communicate as best he could. Ironically, we understood. TC and I had brought Dad a huge card with a picture of Jesus on the card. Dad kept pointing to the card. He would then point to TC and I. He was crying and trying desperately to relay an important message. He seemed to be agitated and unable to rest. The importance of our understanding of what it is he wanted us to know was clearly visible.

I worked hard at trying to figure out his significant message to us. I glanced from the card to the sincere hurt in his face. Finally something clicked. I told my father that not only did God forgive him, but we did as well. We let my father know we loved him. We reassured him we would not abandon him and guaranteed our presence throughout the entire surgery. His facial expression and body movements showed relief at hearing these words. This was the first time I ever saw a sense of peace in his eyes.

TC and I did exactly what we said we would. We stayed in the hospital for almost two days straight. We stayed in the hospital waiting room throughout the entire surgery. We took turns falling asleep as we waited for an update on his condition. Mom called daily seeking information on Dad's condition.

At one point in the surgical process, the doctor came out to the waiting room and informed us that Dad's leg had to be amputated to save his life. The infection had spread and there was no guarantee he would survive. They sought permission to remove his leg and without hesitation Mom gave consent via the telephone.

That night, Dad's leg had successfully been amputated. He was still alive. We both went home to get some much needed rest. Throughout the morning, we had made several calls to the hospital to monitor Dad's condition. He was still alive. It was around noon that the terrible news came from the hospital.

The hospital staff called to inform me that Dad had taken a turn for the worse. He had just suffered a massive heart attack. He was now on life support and was virtually brain dead. The staff further stated Dad was not breathing on his own and was not conscious at all. They told me he would have more heart attacks because his body was ready to shut down. They looked for permission to stop the life support machine if he endured another heart attack. Mom, once again, granted her consent via the telephone.

They asked me to come to the hospital to see my father. At the hospital I was taken into a room with a closed curtain. I entered the enclosed area and saw my father. All signs of life had disappeared from his body. He was dead by all accounts. I learned that between the time of the telephone call from the hospital staff to the time it took me to drive to the hospital, Dad had suffered another heart attack and was gone.

I stood in that room with Dad's body, numb. I wanted to cry, but couldn't. I held his hand for a second. It was cold. I gently touched his face and put my fingers over his eyes. I looked at him, lying there and I asked his lifeless body, "What the hell happened in your life? Why was your soul so tortured?" I began to pray, asking God to give him the peace he so deserved.

Following the funeral, I made a decision to remain with Mom for a while. Jose had been coming to Massachusetts once a month for two days. He was very supportive during the hardship endured during my father's illness and ultimate demise. Nevertheless, this was hardly a way to develop a marriage.

Regardless of this fact, I was much happier with Mom. I had started working a full-time job and was surrounded by my family. Our marriage survived four years like this. I had taken a trip or two to Maryland to spend time with my husband. At one point, I had talked about going back to Maryland with Monique and was quickly discouraged by Jose. He had taken on a roommate who had completely furnished the apartment. Being so pleased at being back home, I decided not to argue the point. I liked my life back home. I just missed my husband.

After three and a half years apart, I gave birth to another child, Nicole. During my pregnancy with Nicole, Jose had expressed an interest in adopting Monique. He absolutely loved and adored her and wanted to legally become her father. Besides, Daniel was not involved in her life at all. I was adamantly opposed to this idea and did not feel it was right. Daniel, on the other hand, was all for it.

He was tired of paying child support and said he would sign over his rights as a parent; thereby allowing Jose to become her legal father. Watching Daniel, unremorsefully sign over his legal rights as a father, caused feelings of massive hurt and pain. Standing in court pregnant, didn't aid in controlling my emotions. To this date, I struggle with forgiving Daniel for abandoning his daughter. Luckily, Jose was a good father to Monique.

Jose was not able to see Nicole until two weeks after she was born. I was basically a single parent again, with a husband.

Shortly after Nicole's birth, a strange visit with Jose occurred. He called and stated he would be taking a train to come stay for the weekend. Monique and I were excited and looked forward to his visit.

Jose came for his visit as promised. Unexpectedly, he announced he could only stay for the afternoon and stated he had been called back to Maryland by the Coast Guard. He called the train station and arranged for his return trip. He was scheduled to leave in two hours. Instinctually, I felt uncomfortable with this situation.

Two hours later, I took Jose to the train station and watched him board the train. He waved goodbye and it was tearful, as usual. I drove back home and went back to my regular routine.

Not long afterward, I received a strange call from Jose. He stated he had gotten off of a train in Connecticut because he discovered the Coast Guard had made a mistake. He did not have to go back. This really didn't sit well with me. I decided to let this situation play itself out before I jumped to conclusions.

Thirty minutes later, my younger brother, Chris, came flying through the door. He began to quiz me, asking if I knew where my husband was. I explained to him that I had taken him to the train station and that he was going back to Maryland. Chris wanted to know if I had actually seen him get on the train. I confirmed that I did and recounted our tearful goodbye. I became confused. Why all the questions? Was there a problem?

Chris hesitated for a moment, and then declared he had something to tell me. His expression indicated this was not easy for him to do. It was killing him to have to give me this information. I prodded and pushed for the information. Chris began explaining he had just come from the shopping mall with his best friend. He and his friend saw my husband in the mall with another woman. They were arm-in-arm and presented as a couple.

I was totally shocked!! Then the anger kicked in. I wanted answers and I wanted them now. I felt like a total fool. I had waited four long years, played the dutiful wife, had no friends and went nowhere, outside of work and home with my children. I started to make a series of telephone calls, beginning with Jose's older brother. I asked him if he had seen his brother and he quickly informed me that he did not want to get involved. Pushing him hard to get some clarity, I managed to elicit some answers I wasn't quite prepared to receive.

I learned Jose had come to town with his girlfriend that he had been living with in Maryland. Jose did not have a roommate, instead he was renting our apartment to a couple. When I went to visit Jose, the couple confirmed Jose's lie indicating he was Jose's roommate and that his girlfriend was just at the apartment visiting.

Jose had created this story about having to go back to Maryland, to create an avenue that would allow him to go between his mother's apartment where he and his girlfriend were staying, to my mother's house where his wife and children were residing.

This information cut like a knife. I knew my older brother, Ricky, had to be aware of the situation. He lived in Maryland and they were both working on the same military base. Why didn't he tell me? Why did he allow me to waste all those years?

I got on the phone and called Jose's mother. His mother spoke in broken English with a heavy Spanish accent. I asked her why she was letting Jose stay at her house with another woman. What kind of mother-in-law was she? She blatantly lied and told me that this woman was just her friend from Maryland. I called her a liar and demanded to speak with her son. She did not know where he was. Ten minutes later, Jose called. He pretended not to know what was transpiring.

I suspected he called to cover his behind, as he knew my

brother saw him in the mall. I began screaming, crying, and demanding answers. He, of course, pretended my brother was a liar. This infuriated my brother. Jose stated he was on his way over to the house to resolve this matter immediately.

I had decided I was due for a night of fun and frolic and began to get myself dressed for the nightclub scene. I had curlers in my hair and a fully made up face. My transformation was beginning to look pretty good. I would show him. Before my new, sexy look had been fully completed, Jose began walking up to the apartment complex.

Chris spotted him as he looked out of the window, hungrily awaiting his approach. He flew down the stairs to greet Jose. Mom and I were right behind him. Chris and Jose began to participate in an explosive exchange of words. I stood in the middle of this argument, hoping to prevent any physical interaction. The argument hit its peak and fists began to fly. As the punches were hurled, I was knocked aside and my curlers were flying out of my hair. To my surprise, Chris put a good spanking on Jose. He firmly told Jose he better dump the girl and take care of his wife and kids.

Jose left the area and attempted to call me several times. Chris intercepted each and every telephone call. I was heartbroken. It wasn't until Jose had gotten back to Maryland and the anger had subsided that I finally had the opportunity to speak to him. Jose said everything I had learned was true and his intentions were to remain in Maryland once he was done with his four years in the Coast Guard.

I could not believe what I was hearing. I felt a huge knot in my stomach as I cried and begged him not to pick her over me and the children. It hurt so badly, I was doubled over, trying to catch my breath. His girlfriend had a lot of money and he enjoyed living that lifestyle he shared with her. He told me he loved me and not her but for now he would be staying with her.

I investigated this situation, and learned several things. The woman that he lived with was employed by the airline that he utilized to fly back and forth between Massachusetts and Maryland. Additionally, she was aware of his marriage but did not care. She stated she was going to keep him in spite of this fact. I wanted to kill this woman. How was she going to keep my husband? I let her know in no uncertain terms that I had the "papers" on his behind and he would be with his wife and kids. I further learned he had several affairs while living in Maryland. There was also a possibility he had another child as a result of one of his affairs. I also discovered he had been unfaithful the entire time I was living in Maryland.

Mom comforted me the best she could during this stressful time in my life. I wanted revenge badly. I wanted to hurt him. My mind entertained all types of violent thoughts. I was educated early in life that violence usually got you what you wanted. Mom, on the other hand, taught me that success is the best revenge. She gently steered my path differently. I started to pray and ask God to help me.

I listened to Mom. I began to put my life together. I had landed myself a decent paying job and found an apartment for myself and the children. I had gotten a car and began to sustain myself and the girls. I had a completely furnished apartment and was feeling a little better.

Jose had now begun to change his mind. He wanted to come home and make things work between us. He wanted to be a father to his children and be a family man. He was truly sorry and never meant to hurt me. I bought it all—hook, line and sinker! During his quest to win his wife back, Jose had gone AWOL (absent without leave), and was imprisoned in a military prison. He was there for a six-month period of time.

I felt to blame for his incarceration. If he hadn't been trying to win me back, he would have never went AWOL. Looking back, I cannot believe how naive and weak I was. Life would teach me lessons—the hard way. After Jose was released from military prison, he was discharged from the Coast Guard.

He came home to his wife and his children. This was one of the biggest mistakes of my entire life. What happened during the last year of our marriage was a nightmare. I got a true glimpse into the evil, sadistic, tortured mind of this man I called my husband.

Not only did this man cheat on me with more women than I can count, he stole money from the household, beat me savagely, and was a big time cocaine user. In addition to this he was stealing cars and selling drugs. He would go to a car lot and pretend to be interested in buying a car. Back then, car dealerships permitted you to take the car off of their lot without a salesman in the car. Jose would take the car and drive to a locksmith and have a copy of the key made. Later on, he would go back to the lot, when the dealership had closed, and drive the car off of the lot. Then he would have the vehicle identification number changed. Then he would resell the car. Of course, I wasn't aware of this at first but it slowly revealed itself.

Jose left me with many memories of our marriage, but there is one particular incident that stands out. It was a Saturday night and Jose was trying to be nice. He took me out to a nightclub. There was a hot new club in town and I was dying to go. The club had three floors and the music was hot. We got to the club and automatically began enjoying ourselves. We had been dancing on the second floor when suddenly I noticed a woman flirting with him. He seemed to be flirting back. I decided to enjoy myself and ignore this slight annoyance. I was just so happy to be out and having fun. I didn't want anything or anyone to spoil this moment. Besides, I had recognized so many people that I had not seen in awhile.

I noticed an irresistibly attractive gentleman. He was handsome to the core. He seemed to be spending a lot of time trying to get my attention. Out of respect for my husband, I pretty much ignored him.

My husband, on the other hand, was entertaining every pretty girl he saw. I started to get fed up with his behavior. The beautiful man who wanted my attention, very respectfully said hello as he walked past me on the dance floor. I casually said hello back to him. My insecure, jealous husband demanded to know who this gentleman was. I told him I did not know. He loudly exclaimed, "How dare you disrespect me! How are you paying attention to other men when you're here with me." I ignored his statement and decided to let this go. That is, until he continued to openly flirt with another woman. I casually asked him who she was. Why did I do that?

Next thing I knew, my husband, in the middle of a crowded club, snatched me off of the dance floor by my hair and dragged me down two flights of stairs. He slapped and punched me all the way down the stairs and out of the door. I mustered a cry for help as he knocked my body into the people standing on the stairs who had been waiting to get onto the dance floor. To my amazement, no one helped me. Not even the club bouncers. People just stood there, shocked, with their mouths hanging open, stating, "Oh, my God."

Once outside of the club, he continued to beat me up. I managed to get away from him and ran as fast as I could to our car. The car was parked behind the club. I jumped in and locked all of the doors. I started up the car and attempted to drive off. I wanted to make an escape but could not drive this particular car. This car was a standard shift and I had not learned how to drive it yet.

Jose was standing outside of the car, banging on the windows, yelling at me to open the door. I was panic stricken and bloody. To my surprise, Jose had a spare key to the car in a small magnetic container on the underside of the car. He began to unlock the door to the car. As he did this, I kept locking the door before he could open it. He would run from door to door unlocking it as I would lock it right back up.

He became infuriated and ran into the alley. He found an old abandoned car bumper and held it over his head. I tried to put the car in reverse but could not figure it out. I just knew he was going to throw that bumper into the car. Fearful of having the glass shatter into my face and possibly getting knocked out by a bumper, I climbed into the back seat and ducked. He took this opportunity to unlock the door and jump into the car.

He snatched me from under the seat and dragged me out of the car and threw me into the front seat. He began to drive the car like a maniac, beating me in the face the entire ride. He parked the car in front of the apartment. The apartment was on the fourth floor.

He kicked, shoved, punched, and dragged me up the entire four flights of stairs. He threw me into the apartment and continued to beat me until my poor little body gave out. I crashed to the floor.

My next memory is of myself sitting in a bathtub full of ice. I could barely hold my head up. He was washing my naked body to remove the dirt and blood that had planted itself all over me. He was giving his speech about how sorry he was and swore he would never hurt me again.

My body ached and I was full of cuts and bruises. I began to tap into my childhood developed skill. I shut off all feeling. I was numb. I refused to cry. I refused to feel. I just existed.

As he continued to apologize and clean me up, he decided he wanted to make love. I did not want him touching me or breathing on me. I was totally disgusted. I knew I could not say no to his desires if I wanted to be alive the next day. I said nothing. I just closed my eyes and shut down my mind. I thought about beautiful beaches and the warm feeling of a beautiful sunrise. I was in another place, imagining a different life. Nothing that was happening at that moment mattered. I wasn't even there. I was in a wonderful place, under the sun.

The beatings continued. I always had bruises, especially underneath my clothing. I took each beating without shedding a tear. I took it like a man. I would not let this man get the best of me. If he killed me, so be it. But he would never get the satisfaction of witnessing shedded tears. This is the one area I refused to grant him control. This did nothing for him, except made him angrier. The black and blue marks on my face were covered with an adequate supply of heavy makeup. I was so oblivious to how badly I looked. People would stare at me with such pity and I couldn't figure out why.

My appearance was so bad at times that I was sent home from work one day by my boss. He saw bruises on my face and strangulation marks on my neck. He took me to the police station and helped me get a restraining order against Jose. At the time, I worked in a locked facility. I was an administrative assistant in a juvenile detention center. All of the staff had been instructed to call the police immediately if he showed up on the premises. This kept him away from the job but not away from me.

I didn't know what to do. I had truly believed it would be a sin to get a divorce. Besides, we were married in the Catholic church. They did not recognize divorce. I felt so trapped. I didn't want my children to be without a father. If I divorced and attempted to have another man or husband in my life, it would be considered adultery. I didn't want to go to hell. If hell was worse than this, then I'd be better off staying where I was.

The extent of Jose's brutality became apparent when he punched his own mother to get at me. He and I were at her apartment, arguing about some woman he had been seen with. He began to threaten physical harm. He came after me and his mother jumped in front of him to prevent him from hurting me. He punched his mother, knocking her backwards.

Seeing this, I got into my car and drove as fast as I could to the police station. He got into his car and followed me all the way to the police station. I got out of my car and attempted to run into the building. He snatched me before I could get close enough for anyone to see what was happening. He proceeded to beat me up outside of the police station. I was convinced I had to devise a plan to get out of this situation.

I started focusing my attention on my finances. I struggled to stay on top of my bills. I was unable to save any money because I was the funding source for every bill or expense we had. I had learned that Jose was selling drugs. He would come home with wads of cash and drop it in front of me. I refused to take any of his money. I told him it was drug money and I would rather suffer than take tainted money. He told me I was a fool.

As a matter of fact, everyone thought I was nuts. I could not bring myself to take that money. I tried to be obedient to what I felt God wanted me to do.

Jose had begun to stay away from the house for days at a time. In some senses this was a relief and in another sense it was frustrating. It kept me at a standstill, not allowing me to get on with my life. Rumors were spreading about an older woman that Jose had supposedly been dating.

I found this difficult to believe because the woman was so much older and not really attractive at all. The only thing that might lend credibility to the rumor was that she had money. Jose liked money. It was also rumored that Jose was dating his cousin who had just moved to the area from Puerto Rico. I didn't give much credibility to this because she was his cousin. Would he actually be seeing his cousin? Hmmmm. I decided to investigate both situations.

Inevitably, I discovered it was all pretty much true. But it was far worse than I could imagine. One day there was a knock on my door. Jose was home and things were pretty quiet. I answered the door and standing there were Jose's cousin and the older woman. They had both come to my house to tell me they had both been in a relationship with my husband. The older woman announced she was pregnant by my husband and his cousin announced she had just lost his baby a week ago.

My mind snapped. His clothing began flying out of the fourth floor window. I ordered him and his two b------ out of my house. That was it! I got another restraining order and I believe he knew I meant business. It was at this time that I wanted to hurt him badly. I tried to run him down with my car. I scratched my name in his car with my keys. I dared him to lift a hand towards me.

He pretty much left me alone. That is, until he was served with divorce papers. He had the nerve to try to talk me out of this. During this time, he had been living with his cousin and her children. I ignored him and began to put my life together. Just when I felt confident in what I was doing, he threw a major monkey wrench in my plan. He told me that regardless of whether or not I got a divorce, I was still his wife. He reminded me that we were married in the Catholic church and they would continue to recognize our marriage.

This hit me hard, because he was basically right. He knew how I felt about my faith and how I tried to live my life with morals and values. My confidence was knocked down, hard. I could not give up or give in to this brute. I decided to make an appointment with the church priest and tell him everything.

I needed help. I had to get out of this situation. I met with the priest of my church and revealed everything about my marriage to him. To my relief, I was told to go ahead and get the divorce legally and at the same time he would assist me in obtaining an annulment of my marriage through the church diocese. The priest told me that no one should be subjected to the things I had been going through and that God would not want me to remain in this situation. It felt as if a huge burden had been lifted off of my shoulders. I was eager to get on with this. I wanted to close this chapter of my life forever.

I knew I had been damaged goods. I had contracted a sexually transmitted disease that would affect the rest of my life. The disease was an inflammation of the pelvic (PID—pelvic inflammatory disease) area that could inevitably cause infertility. It caused a great deal of pain to the pelvic area. It was treated with antibiotics if caught early enough. I thought I had overcome this problem but realized later on in life, it had never gone away.

This disease was contracted not only as a result of Jose's many adulterous affairs but also as a result of the type of sexual activities he had me engage in with him. I will not elaborate on details as it relates to this area of my life. But I will say I never thought his sexual desires were normal. I just believed I had to do what my husband wanted sexually, whether I liked it or not. I thought this was part of my role as his wife. Unfortunately, this disease would impact my entire life.

I had finally gotten the divorce on the grounds of cruel and abusive treatment. I had retained custody of the children and attempted to get some sort of child support. Jose managed to get around this situation by claiming he had no income. The judge ordered he pay only $50 a month for two children until he obtained a job.

Here I was, a single mother with two children, a limited income and basically no child support. This man had abused me for years, cheated on me, etc. and didn't have to be responsible for anything or anybody. I had been left in debt of over $20,000.

In the middle of this mess, I had learned Jose had been stealing money from my bank account. He was doing this in conjunction with stealing my credit cards and charging them to their maximum limit. I had just recently deposited $5,000 into my bank account. This is money I had obtained from an income tax return. I had eagerly waited for this money. I was trying to get myself financially stable and back on track. I wrote out checks to cover all the household expenses.

To my amazement, I received notification from the bank informing me I had bounced a substantial number of checks. I was totally confused and knew it had to be a mistake. I was asked to come to the bank immediately to clear up this matter. Meanwhile, I was incurring an added fee of $25 for every check that bounced.

I walked into the bank with my receipt indicating I had deposited $5,000. I was totally confident this would be cleared up quickly. The bank manager took the receipt I had produced, stating she would be right back. I waited for some time for the manager to return. When she returned, the manager informed me that someone had been using my ATM card and pulling funds out of my account.

I was totally perplexed. I knew no one had access to this account besides myself. She further stated all ATM transactions are recorded. The manager would send for the videotapes of the recordings for the days in questions. She told me it would take three days before she had obtained them all.

Three days later, I went back to the bank to view the videotapes. As she began playing the tapes, my heart dropped to my feet. She asked me if I recognized the individual on the tape. Tape after tape after tape was my soon-to-be ex-husband pulling all of my money out of the bank via the ATM machine. He was smiling and waving at a woman who was waiting for him in a car outside of the bank. It was Jose and his cousin.

The bank manager told me there was not much they could do. I told her I was in the process of obtaining a divorce and he had stolen my ATM card out of my purse and figured out my pin number. The woman told me they might help me if I would be willing to press charges. Without hesitation, I told her to press charges.

I recovered some of my money and really had a difficult time repairing this mess. I was now financially strapped and had no clue as to how I was going to manage. It was only by God's grace we survived.

Jose was every bit of my father. This marriage helped me to better understand the trauma my mother had endured. I felt a greater appreciation for her. I started to search for healing and repair to my broken heart. As usual, I wanted a quick fix to this problem. I continued to search for some spiritual revelation. My road to self-discovery and self-healing began.

Chapter Six

Self-healing

FOLLOWING THE DIVORCE, I had a lot of work to do in my life if I wanted things to change. I was tired of being this needy person. I was hungry for any information I could find, any book I could read that would help me heal from this situation.

I felt much more compassion for my mother as I could really relate to what she had endured in her own life. I was eager to get some insight into my parents' backgrounds. I had a strong desire to get a better understanding of what happened to them as children.

I began to investigate and learned things about both of my parents that shed some light on what had happened during my childhood. My paternal grandmother was a mother of ten children and had been married for several years. Her husband inevitably passed away, leaving her a widow. She lived in North Carolina and was a successful store owner. Twenty years after her husband's death, she closed the store and moved to the state of Florida.

In Florida she met a man who had also been a widower for some time. He had a successful logging business. This man was white and his former wife had been black. My grandmother believed this man would marry her. She gave birth to my father but he never married her.

Disappointed, my grandmother left the state of Florida and moved to New York. My grandmother did not want to take my father, her newborn son, with her. His complexion was fair and he did not look like her other ten children.

My grandmother decided she was going to wrap my father up in a blanket and leave him in a corner of a building. Luckily for my father, people noticed she had left Florida but did not have a baby with her. A woman found my father in the building and decided to raise him as her own. My father had always been told that his mother had died.

When my father was nine years of age, the woman who raised him introduced him to his mother. His mother had learned he was alive and being raised by this woman in Florida. She decided to come back and get him. My father was shocked to learn his mother was not dead.

My grandmother took him back to New York with her. Life for him became very hard. My father was never accepted by his half siblings, mainly because he looked different. My grandmother was mean to him and would often neglect him.

My father was very angry and confused and began to get into trouble. He became very rebellious. At a young age, my father would hang around the Apollo Theater in New York. This was not the ideal place for a young child to hang around. Musicians were infamous for their wild lifestyles and their involvement with drugs. My father was exposed to this atmosphere very early in his life. Most importantly, he felt acceptance. He was starving for acceptance, especially since he wasn't getting it at home.

The musicians loved him. Billy Eckstine, a famous jazz singer, decided to take my father under his wing. I was told that he had such an interest in my father that at the age of 13 he took my father to court and legally had his name changed to Eckstine. Legally, my father had been given the name of a famous jazz legend.

My father began to travel with Billy and his band and would at times sit in for him and sing for him. My father and Billy incredibly looked alike and sang exactly the same. My father actually made recordings for Billy. He had a wonderful voice.

My father continued to get into trouble, as he was still dealing with his childhood and issues of anger. He got caught up in the fast lifestyle and the drugs early on. He and Billy eventually had a falling out and Billy separated himself from my father. Billy felt my father was disgracing his name by his troublesome behaviors. He remained angry with my father for quite awhile.

This, of course, is the story I've been told my entire life. I have also been told a very different version of the same story. It's also been said that my father lied and legally changed his name himself and began committing crimes and was ordered away from Billy, because of his behaviors. I've never known which version is true but based on Dad's history, the latter is most likely the truth.

It wasn't until my father turned 29 years of age did he actually learn the identity of his true father. His mother told him he had two older sisters living in New York whom he finally met. My father had some memories of his father when he was a little boy being raised in Florida just before his mother retrieved him. He remembered a man who would come to the house and take him to his logging business. He interacted with this man and his children and enjoyed himself. He had no idea that these people were actually his biological family members.

All throughout my life, Dad expressed his hatred of white people. He would refer to white people as devils, among other things. I found it strange, because he had white friends. I never understood what that was about, until I learned of his background. In retrospect, it was apparent that my father never hated white people, but was incredibly angry at the part of him that was rejected by his own mother. His mother made him feel bad about who he was because he was different than his siblings. His siblings fed into this notion instilled in them by their mother. Because his being half white was a source of great pain and rejection, my father hated that part of himself.

My siblings and I did not like our grandmother at all. My father expressed his hatred of his mother quite often. Despite his very vocal expression of hatred towards his mother, Dad always made it a point to visit her every time we took a trip to New York.

His mother never liked his children. That was obvious. We were very light in complexion and she pointed this out every chance she could get. My father seemed to always want to please her. He never accomplished this task.

Learning this about him helped to alleviate some of my own anger towards him and provided me with some insight as to his behaviors. It never fully admonished him from the hurt and pain he had caused. But it enabled me to find forgiveness.

My mother came from a totally different upbringing. She has some very fond memories of her parents and her upbringing. Her parents were second cousins and entered into an arranged marriage. Unfortunately, her mother died at the age of 35. I was always told, growing up, that my grandmother had died of pneumonia. I later learned the truth.

My mother has seven siblings, one of which is her twin sister. My grandmother struggled over the years with depression. She was very close to her own mother and each time she became pregnant she wanted to go back to the islands to be close to her.

During my grandmother's last pregnancy, she had planned a trip to the islands to be with her mother again. Her mother had been traveling by boat from St. Kitts to St. Barts and midway through this trip there was an explosion on board. Her mother perished in this explosion. This triggered a severe depression for her. It was already determined that she had been struggling with postpartum depression. But this event triggered a far more severe depression for her.

Her depression had gotten so severe that she had to be institutionalized. My grandfather came home one day looking for my mother's youngest brother. He was just an infant. My grandmother informed him that she had given him to the nuns because she couldn't take care of him. My grandfather tracked him down to the Guardian Angel Home. He remained in this home for some time. My grandfather realized something had to be done. He went before a judge who in turn committed her to the institution for a three-month period.

Upon her hospitalization, Mom and her twin sister were sent to live with their aunt. Their younger sister had already been staying there. Her brothers remained at home with my grandfather. My grandfather had to work and the boys were older and much more self-sufficient.

After Grandmother's three-month stay at the hospital, my grandfather went to the hospital to bring her home. Grandpa desperately wanted his family back together. My grandmother had overdosed on pills and lapsed into a coma. She died before my grandfather had a chance to bring her back home.

Following my grandmother's suicide, the children were all separated again. Mom and her twin sister were sent to live with a family by the name of "Wells." This was the family of the woman who cared for my grandmother while she had been hospitalized. She was my grandmother's nurse.

My mother's youngest sister remained in the home of her aunt. The three boys stayed with their father. The baby remained in the Guardian Angel Home.

The Wells were an extremely religious family. My mother and her sister were heavily restricted. They were not allowed to wear makeup or listen to music. Sundays were spent entirely in church. In the morning, my mother and her sister were allowed to go to Catholic church (that is the faith they were raised in) and the rest of the day was spent in the church of the Wells family.

The nuns at the Guardian Angel Home had informed my grandfather that he had better find a way to get the baby back or he would be put up for adoption. My grandfather was desperate to have all of his children together, so he presented my grandmother's nurse with a proposal.

He asked Ms. Wells if she would be willing to marry him to prevent the baby from being adopted. This would enable him to get all of his children back. He told Ms. Wells if she wanted to get a divorce afterwards that would not become an issue. Ms. Wells agreed to this and my mother and her siblings were all back home. Ms. Wells and my grandfather never got a divorce.

My mother and her siblings lived rather well. They had a decent home and were well provided for. They were raised under the same strict religious doctrine that the Wells family had exposed she and her sister to.

The rules were so strict they were ridiculous. By the time my mother and her sister were ready to go to college, they were vulnerable and completely unskilled in relationships. My mother was not allowed to date until she turned 21 years of age. Thereby, making her easy prey for my father.

Learning this helped me to understand why my mother felt it so important families stay together. My mother wanted her children to have a father and had very strong feelings about separation in families. In addition, her strong religious background definitely added to her thinking about marriage. It was her belief that you stay married, no matter what.

Now, I needed to discover how I could stop my own addiction to toxic relationships. I continued to find a safe haven within my weekly visit to church. But, I wasn't getting what I needed and wanted a better understanding of how God could help me.

Following the divorce, I lived the single life for close to four years. I was never without a date and always had some interested male calling me. I was hard as nails and had put up a huge wall. I would literally push men out of my life before a relationship had a chance to develop. I wasn't willing to place any type of trust in anyone, especially with my heart.

On the outside, I presented as a very put together person. Inside, I was a broken, shattered mess. Fragile as a delicate flower fighting to keep its petals in a violent windstorm.

I hated being single. It never felt comfortable or comforting for me. I secretly longed for the stability found in a solid, committed relationship. I felt trapped between two worlds; the lie I was portraying versus the empty, lonely person on the inside.

Being alone was torturous for me. Being alone, meaning, without anyone in the room or around me. If I wasn't taking care of someone or around a group of people, I felt totally lost. It was a sad sight to see. If my children weren't home and I was left home alone, I was a mess. I would either call everyone I knew until I found someone who was willing to entertain me, or get in my car and find someone to be around.

I never allowed myself any quality time with myself. I couldn't sit still long enough to learn the lesson life was attempting to teach me. The books I had been reading helped me to identify my issues. I could tell you exactly what was wrong with me and what I needed to do to deal with the feelings I had inside. I just could not find enough peace within myself to begin to apply anything I had learned or read about to my life.

I believed I was fighting off the inner demons that tormented me. I was dependent on others to provide me with the love I was never able to feel for myself. At times, I would convince myself that I had it all together. Just under the surface, lay the truth.

From time to time, I would experience nightmares and flashbacks of the terrible abuse I had suffered; waking up from a tortured sleep with sweat pouring off of me, stifling screams in order to not wake the children. I had educated myself on domestic violence issues and post-traumatic stress disorder. I was fully aware of the fact that I was suffering with this.

Seeing a therapist was not an option for me. I felt I could handle this myself. I would continue to read, study, pray and not deny what was going on inside of me. I told myself I would rely on God to bring what He felt I needed. I could never sit still long enough to appreciate God's work. Besides, He took too long for me. I had no patience. Just as quick as I convinced myself I had "given it to God," I would quickly create my own situations and convince myself that it was probably God working in my life. It never was God at that time. It was always me.

Then, when things didn't work out the way I thought they should, I got mad at God. I would pray the funniest prayers back then. I would close my eyes with my list of things I wanted God to give me. I would say crazy things like:

Dear God,

Please bring me a decent man in my life. Please make sure he's not ugly and I don't want a man that cheats. Can you make sure he doesn't beat me. He can have some kids, because I have kids and think that would be okay. I don't care if he smokes but I don't want a man who does drugs. I like men that are slender and tall and not fat and chunky. Please don't give me a man with a gut. That is so nasty. And please God could you make sure he is...

This went on with several requests for what I thought I wanted and needed. I definitely needed some work. I also needed to learn what God was really about. I don't think God faulted me because I was naive. My heart was in it.

I knew I had low self-esteem and I recognized my patterns

and codependent behaviors. I learned how to journal my thoughts and feelings which I found quite healing.

I started to focus on building a career. I enrolled myself in college and successfully earned a degree in the field of court reporting. I had landed a job as soon as I completed my education. I had gained some self-esteem and was beginning to feel good about myself; at least in this area of my life. I was the first member of my family to earn a college degree and this gave me some sense of pride.

The field of court reporting can be very interesting at times. I was working in superior court and involved in some heavy-duty cases. It was one month into my career and I was the reporter on a case that involved an attempted murder charge. My case involved a prostitute/crack addict, who had given birth via cesarean section two weeks prior to the alleged crime. The prostitute had taken her customer to a remote outdoor area, hidden by shrubbery. The alleged customer had taken a very long pair of garden shears, and plunged them into the prostitute and opened them up. I can't begin to tell you the damage caused to this woman. It was amazing to see her still alive and testifying on the witness stand.

This was an ideal career for me. I found law interesting and was attracted to drama and chaos. I had a coworker who was working on a case in an adjacent courtroom. Her case involved an accident that led to the severing of the leg of a motorcyclist. During our breaks or downtime, she and I would share information about our cases and view the exhibits.

I showed her the long garden shears and pictures of the victim's scars and injuries she suffered as a result of this heinous act inflicted upon her. My coworker, in turn, showed me photographs of the motorcycle smashed up and the severed leg lying in the highway.

We had both endured a trying day and our brains felt totally fried. At the end of the day, we packed up our equipment and headed for home. My coworker lived nearby and she usually walked home. I offered her a ride home. I recognized that even though the walk home for her wasn't bad, carrying all of her equipment while walking could be burdensome. She gladly took the ride.

I pulled up in front of the condominium complex she lived in. My car had been pulled over, onto the curb, parked. This was a two-lane street and traffic was usually heavy. We sat in the car for several minutes, discussing the day's events. As we were talking, I kept feeling a compulsion to look in my rearview mirror.

We were wrapping up our conversation. My coworker had opened the car door, getting ready to step out of the car. At the same time, I noticed a truck getting close to the back of the car. The driver was not looking ahead of him and seemed to be fiddling around with his radio. I saw pictures in my mind of that leg lying in the road from her accident case.

I grabbed my coworker and shouted, "We're going to get hit!" Sure enough, that truck slammed directly into the back of my car. Upon impact, she and I slammed forward, my chest plunging into the steering wheel. Then, the car began flipping over. She and I began to pray, loudly, and held on for dear life.

The car stopped flipping over and ended up lying on its side (driver's side flat with the ground). Neither one of us could get ourselves out of that car. Fortunately, passersby worked hard to get us out of that car. Unbelievably, after we had been pulled out of the car, we were able to walk away with barely a scratch.

We were transported by ambulance to the hospital. We were extremely shaken up but felt overall pretty good. That is, until the next day. Both she and I were back in the emergency room the next morning. Whiplash had set in and my chest was killing me. X-rays were taken of my back to ensure the metal rod placed there during my previous surgery was still in its proper place.

Thankfully, the rod was intact, but I was now experiencing back and neck pain. I was out of work for a short period of time. I began receiving intensive physical therapy and had been prescribed several different medications (none of which I took). I began to realize this newfound career may be short lived.

The job itself entailed sitting for several hours in front of a machine, recording each and every word spoken. Some days were worked without a break. This was an incredible strain on the neck and back and made for a very long day.

Simultaneously, the PID (pelvic inflammatory disease) that I thought had been successfully treated was beginning to manifest itself with noticeable symptoms. The symptoms got progressively worse rather quickly. Over the course of several years, I had been experiencing very sharp pain in the pelvic area. This pain could stop me dead in my tracks. The pain would last for a very brief period of time and then disappear. The pain was not consistent and would come every now and then.

I never thought it required any medical treatment until the pain had started to become consistent. This pain would be so excruciating that it would not permit me to stand in an upright position. When the pain was present, I could not walk with any smoothness or fluidity.

When I initially sought medical treatment, I was given pain medication and scheduled for exploratory surgery. The surgery revealed the PID had never gone away. I had developed major scar tissue and some of it was removed during the surgery, I was informed by my doctor that I was in all probability infertile.

The plan was to wait to see if the removal of scar tissue would help to control the pain. The pain never left and the medications continued to be prescribed. I took the medication only if absolutely necessary. I did not want any type of addiction to any type of drug. In order to prevent this, I endured a lot of pain.

I had decided to take a hiatus from any form of dating. My children were in Chicago, spending the summer with Scherrie and her family. I was left here, totally alone. I hated being alone. I missed my children desperately and was bored to death.

I had convinced myself, up to this point, that I had healed myself. No longer would I allow anyone to abuse me or treat me badly. I felt I was so much stronger and wiser. Little did I know, I would once again prove myself wrong. I couldn't appreciate just how vulnerable I really was. I was on the verge of discovering just how far I had come and how much farther I had to go.

Chapter Seven

Always the Bride, Rarely the Bridesmaid

IT WAS APPROXIMATELY THREE years after my divorce from Jose that I encountered Rashawn. It was just by chance that I met him. I honestly was not looking to meet anyone. My sister, who lived in the townhouse apartment across from my own, recognized my boredom with not having the children home with me. She invited me on an outing with herself and her friends.

With much apprehension, I embarked on this little adventure. Besides, what harm could it do? To my surprise, I ended up having a good time. It was on this outing that I was introduced to Rashawn.

Rashawn wasn't really the type of guy I usually dated or found myself attracted to. But, I was taken by our conversation. In the early stages of our relationship, he presented very well on the surface. Either that, or I was just totally blinded by stupidity.

Nevertheless, he started the relationship with several lies. It took some months before I discovered his facade. By this time, I had already become invested in working this out. I had felt a failure in all of my previous relationships and was determined to stick this one out.

In the "getting to know you better" process, he had told me he was a psychologist at a treatment facility for children. He wore a professional badge around his neck that would lead one to believe what he said. I quizzed him somewhat, because I didn't have much trust for anyone. I asked him about his college education and degree. He provided a story that sounded very credible.

He went on to talk about his involvement with his two sons and expressed much love for his children. This really impressed me, because my daughters had uninvolved fathers.

Jose had dropped out of the girls' lives for several years now, causing major hurt and pain. The first few months after the divorce, he had spent every other weekend with his daughters. He had married his cousin (I later learned she wasn't his blood cousin) and created several other children.

Child support had been after him, not only as it related to my children, but for the child of the older woman he had an affair with. The last time my daughters saw him was on a Christmas day. He came to the apartment with new bicycles and jewelry for the girls. He told me he was going to Puerto Rico for a while but would be back soon. He told me child support was after him and some woman had pressed charges against him for beating her up. That was the last we would see of him for a while.

It really hurt me badly. I managed to put my feelings about how he had treated me during our marriage aside for the sake of my children. I never spoke badly of their father and encouraged their relationship. I swallowed my anger and would spend time at his home and participated in family functions with he, his new wife, and their kids. People who knew our history thought I had lost my mind.

But, it didn't matter what they thought about this. I was willing to sacrifice whatever I had to in order to enable my children to have a relationship with their father. My children loved him then and I didn't want them in the middle, having to feel conflicted about loyalty issues.

I wasn't receiving child support of any kind. You would think for $50 a month, he would have at least tried to pay that. Nope, nothing! It was difficult to see him raising all those other children (two of which were not his) and not providing for our girls. I suppressed my anger, my hurt, my feelings for the benefit of my kids. I don't know if they can ever appreciate how huge a sacrifice that was for me. His disappearance was very traumatic for my children.

Now, I had a man in front of me, speaking what sounded like a foreign language. This man sounded like he always made time for his sons. He wasn't the type of father who dropped off gifts or did his duty and kept his kids whenever he felt like it. He knew about his children's schoolwork, their medical needs, their likes and dislikes. Wow! I was impressed.

He lived at home with his mother and grandmother. He explained he did so because they were both sick and he helped care for them. He didn't have a car, but said it was involved in a recent car accident and had been destroyed. He wasn't a party person and didn't seem to be a womanizer.

In the early stages of our relationship, I was taken on several dates. Rashawn always had enough money to cover expenses for each outing or event. He had a knack for writing poetry and spoke about current world events. He presented as someone much different than I was used to and I was initially impressed.

Our dating continued throughout the summer. At summer's end, I took a trip to Chicago to bring my children back home. My children had heard about Rashawn but were cautious and not very interested in getting to know him.

It took some time before I met his children and he met mine. It wasn't long after everyone met each other that things began to deteriorate and truths started to surface. What was initially perceived as wonderful qualities, revealed themselves as half-truths and pretty packaging. What lied beneath the surface was far more troubling.

Over time, I learned Rashawn was not a psychologist. He was actually working a part-time position as a relief worker. He had lost his job early on and pretended he was going to work everyday. He never had a car but was truthful about being involved in an accident. It was his cousin's car and he had been a passenger. As a result of the accident, he had received settlement money to compensate for his injuries.

This explained why he didn't seem to lack finances. The settlement money wasn't significant and was depleted quickly. He didn't do anything productive with it. He seemed to have no sense of what being a responsible man meant.

He had no college education but was intelligent. His poetry was pretty good but he never did anything with it. He never seemed to possess enough confidence to believe in his work. As a result of his lack of confidence and self-esteem, the poetry sat in a box, collecting dust.

Rashawn was a "momma's boy" who was still at his mother's beck and call. His children were always dropped off at his mother's house and any plans he may have had were always interrupted. He and I would try to plan an event or outing and it would always be interrupted just before we got out of the door. The phone would ring and sure enough it would either be his mother or grandmother telling him he needed to come home immediately. His children were there and they wanted to see their father.

He never had the courage to say anything other than, "I'll be right there." This would be the source of many arguments. He definitely was dealing with "baby momma drama," which really got on my nerves. It was quite apparent that all parties were desperately trying to sabotage the relationship before it had a chance to get off of the ground.

This was the perfect opportunity for me to tap into my role

as caretaker for everyone else. I had this incredible skill for taking on people's problems and issues as my own. I would begin my mission to become the savior of the heavy burdened. I never saw my own need to be saved from myself. Instead, I put all my energies into making things better for everyone else. Neglect of my own need to care for myself took a toll on my own well-being.

I felt sorry for him and was determined to help this man whom I saw as a victim. He expressed his exhaustion at being at their whims and desires. He took a stand and moved into his cousin's apartment. The apartment itself was a mess. He blamed this sloppiness on his cousin. He would spend a lot of time at my apartment; much more than he did at his own apartment.

Once I learned Rashawn had lost his job due to layoffs, I encouraged him to get unemployment benefits until he could get a job. He was adamantly opposed to this idea. He let me know this was beneath him. I was stunned. I couldn't understand how someone with no income and children to support and rent to pay thought he was above receiving unemployment benefits. He always had this superior attitude. He acted like he was better than everyone else.

He acted this way in terms of his children also. He often spoke about how wonderful they were but would always point out my children's flaws. This did not sit well with me, so his time with his children was spent mainly at his mother's house or his own apartment. This created more controversy among his family members. They were under the impression that I did not like his children or were jealous of his kids.

It had nothing to do with jealousy. It was about not having my children subjected to anything or anyone that would make them feel bad about who they were. In addition, I was always pushing and encouraging him to help out his children's mother with finances. I would ask about their well-being often and took a real interest in them. The stage had been set by Rashawn to indicate I was the villain. I let people believe whatever they were told. I didn't make it my job to change their minds.

He was very insecure and would get upset if I said hello to someone I used to date. It made him upset just knowing I had a past before he came along. I found this ridiculous. At least he didn't have to deal with any drama from Jose. He had disappeared. But I was faced with his drama quite often. I did not care about his former life. But we were different in that respect.

His insecurities were phenomenal and revealed their magnitude by a very traumatic incident. Rashawn and I were invited to a New Year's Eve party given by a couple I had befriended. Several people were invited, including a roommate of a former boyfriend of mine. No big deal, right? Wrong.

Apparently, in a casual conversation between Rashawn and the roommate, the roommate acknowledged he knew me. He didn't elaborate how he knew me. He just mentioned we knew each other. Rashawn was very aware of who he was and how I knew him and he also knew he would be attending the party.

As a result of this simple exchange, Rashawn developed a major attitude during the party. His mood change was very apparent to everyone at the party. He expressed his desire to leave the party—NOW. I was enraged at his nonsense. Partygoers looked confused at his behavior and so did I. I had no idea what his problem was and why he wanted to leave. I had not been in the room when he had this simple exchange of words.

He began to incite an argument at the party. He wasn't loud, but it was obvious to anyone watching that there was a disagreement taking place. I made up some lame excuse and left the party with him. We sat outside in the car for a little while as I quizzed him as to what exactly was wrong with him.

He told me he was sick and tired of being reminded of my

past. I told him how ludicrous he sounded. He got eerily quiet and I began to drive the car to my apartment. The party was around the corner from my apartment, so we were there in no time.

Fortunately, my children were not at home and were spending the night at my sister's apartment which was in the same complex. Once inside the apartment, his disposition changed to that of a complete stranger. He yelled and hollered and called me terrible names. He called me a tramp, a whore and a slut. He blamed me for upsetting him. He spoke so fast and was full of fury that he was literally foaming at the mouth.

I quickly began to walk up the stairs, away from him. I told him to get out of my house. I further informed him that the relationship was over and I never wanted to see him again. He replied with a nasty remark. He stated, "Go ahead and be the tramp that you are. I'm sure you'll find another man soon because that's what hot ass b------ like you do."

That was it! I was sick of listening to this filthy talk and would not subject myself to another insult. I turned around, looked directly at him standing at the bottom of the stairs, smirked the nastiest smirk I could and calmly said, "I will. No problem."

Why in the world did I say that? This man ran up those stairs so fast he practically flew. He lunged at me placing a very firm grip on my neck. He dragged me to the bed with both of his hands around my neck. I had been choked before and figured this would be over soon.

To my surprise, his grip became firmer and I struggled to breathe. I tried with all my might to get his hands off of my neck. He was too powerful and I couldn't loosen his grip. I began to pray really hard for God to spare my life. My children had lost their father and would be devastated if they had no mother.

My legs had been kicking and I couldn't fight him off

anymore. I can't even begin to describe the incredible fear and panic I felt. I saw death before my very own eyes. I began to lose consciousness and just in the nick of time, he let go of my neck.

I gasped for any morsel of air I could get. I coughed and choked as my throat became familiar with air again. I tried for quite some time to collect myself and finally got some leverage. He was lying in the bed next to me with his hands on his head, yelling, "Why, why?"

Next thing I knew, he rolled over near my face and sunk his teeth into my cheek really hard. The force of his teeth was incredibly painful. His jaws remained clenched in my face for what seemed to be hours. He released the grip of his teeth and jumped off of the bed and ran into the bathroom.

I was overwhelmed with shock and fear. I needed to get out of here fast and get some help before he killed me. I was so petrified I couldn't move. He acted like a crazed animal and I couldn't predict his next move.

He came out of the bathroom with a bottle of pain pills, announcing he was going to swallow them and kill himself. Oh, how I wanted him to kill himself. He poured the entire bottle of pills into his mouth and began swallowing. Pure instinct kicked in and I yanked open his mouth and stuck my fingers down his throat. This caused him to regurgitate some of the pills. I didn't want his dead body on my hands.

For the remainder of the evening, until the late morning hours, I was stuck in that room with this nut. I kept quiet and still. I listened to him babble about being sorry for what had just happened. He went on with his speech about not wanting to lose me, blah, blah, blah.

Because of the irrational nature of his behavior, I said whatever I could to keep him from getting agitated. This lasted for nine long hours. I began to notice he was getting tired and figured he had ingested some of the pills which were beginning to take effect. I coaxed him into closing his eyes and getting some rest. I prayed he would fall asleep.

He eventually fell asleep. I was afraid to move until I was really sure he was out of it. I looked out of the window and saw my sister pull up to her apartment with my daughters. I crept down the stairs and got out of the door without incident.

My children saw me and I quickly stopped them from running close enough to see any damage that may be visible. I motioned for my sister to direct the kids into her apartment. She quickly got them inside and told them to stay there until we came and got them. She could sense something was wrong and we slowly started walking towards each other.

As my sister got closer, her eyes widened and she blurted out, "Oh, my God! What the ---- happened?" I explained quickly what I had just endured. I whispered he was still inside asleep and that I had snuck out. I was stunned and dazed and didn't know what to do. My sister sensed my inability to function properly and began taking care of business.

She immediately sent the children upstairs and put on their favorite movie and gave them a special treat. She brought me into the apartment and immediately called the police. The police came quicker than I expected and I felt relief and shame.

I let them into the apartment and they removed him from the apartment in handcuffs. He was arrested and taken to the police station. I was then placed into a separate car and transported to the police station where I was photographed and interviewed. I was so humiliated and embarrassed.

I thought of my career as a court reporter. I often worked with police officers and judges in my line of work and was well known among court officials. The thought of having to reveal all of this in a courtroom seemed like the worse thing on the planet.

When I saw the photographs of myself, in that condition, the reality of how close to death I came was frightening. I had hemorrhaging in both eyes and the imprint of his entire jaw was embedded in my face. My neck had obvious strangulation marks and you could visibly see the outline of his fingers.

To add insult to injury, his family blamed me for his assault. Their response was that he was probably stressed out about arguing about the children. I couldn't believe what I was hearing. I was so hurt. He owned no responsibility for his behavior. He lied to his family and even to my friends about how things happened. I was crushed.

I sank into a deep depression, feeling I was doomed to this type of treatment. He and I stayed apart for a period of time after this incident. This was the most confusing time in my life. I couldn't see anything clearly. I led myself to believe everyone was against me and I was a failure. I was ashamed of my life and fed into my own frustrations.

Eventually, I allowed Rashawn back into my life. There is no rhyme or reason for it. It just was something I felt compelled to do. I was at a low point in my life and it felt like I just gave up and gave in. I lied to everyone about how he had gotten treatment and therapy. I told them I was confident this would never happen again. I did whatever I could to cover up my own craziness.

It wasn't long afterwards that we were married. I had already gone through several surgeries for the PID and was slated to have another major surgery two weeks after the wedding. This added to my own negative feelings about myself. I felt like damaged goods and resigned myself to believe no one would want me. Sex was out of the question (it was too painful) and I would never have children again. I felt Rashawn was the best I could do in my life. I never really loved him, but I did marry him.

I remember my wedding day very well. I couldn't believe I was actually considering this. The event was designed to be a gala event. The ceremony itself was going to be gorgeous. The reception was slated to be the family event of the year. Everyone was excited and looking forward to this affair. Everyone that is, except me. I knew I shouldn't be marrying this man.

I knew our problems would only get worse. I just didn't have the courage to admit I had made another huge mistake. I felt I had to see it through. Deep down inside, I had resigned myself to believe I would never find a relationship that would bring me happiness. I thought this was the best I was going to get.

I walked down that aisle in the most gorgeous wedding dress I could find. I felt like Miss America walking the runway. As I walked down the church aisle, I heard many comments about how wonderful I looked. I was relishing this attention. The last thing on my mind was the reality of what was waiting for me at the end of the aisle.

I stood next to my fiancé and immediately wanted to run away. I felt trapped with nowhere to go but to the hell I faced by marrying this man. I had a difficult time repeating my vows. I stuttered and had to start over several times. I managed to get through it despite my difficulty.

I had done it. All I could think about was what everyone would think if I got divorced. I remember riding in the limousine, not wanting to kiss or be near my groom. I tolerated the ride until we got to the reception hall.

The hall was perfect. The reception party was phenomenal. Everyone had a fabulous time. Rashawn's sons and my daughters were a part of the ceremony. Everything was picture perfect on the outside. The real picture was much different on the inside.

It wasn't ten minutes after we had arrived home from the ceremony, when the telephone rang. He and I never had a honeymoon, as I was slated for surgery in two weeks. He answered the telephone, and the drama began. Instead of focusing on his bride, he spent an hour on the telephone arguing with the mother of his children. I realized at that moment, just how big a mistake I had made.

Two weeks following the ceremony, I had entered the hospital for the completion of the hysterectomy I had several years prior. The surgery went well and I healed rather quickly. I learned that my insides were so badly damaged that I had major scar tissue among other things. My intestines were stuck together and had to be separated, as well as my appendix removed. I had no ovaries left and had to begin hormone replacement therapy.

I was released from the hospital two days later, despite some hesitation from the medical professionals. The biggest area of concern was the functioning of my intestines. The first week at home was miserable. I could not hold any food down and I was extremely weak. Family members were a big support. Rashawn, on the other hand, made things difficult.

Once my condition had stabilized and I was able to handle food, family members went back to their regular routines and tended to their families. I had been instructed by the doctor that I would need to heal for approximately six weeks. This meant, I was not allowed to go up and down stairs and rest was a key element in my recovery.

Unfortunately, I found myself going up and down the stairs, and handling the household as if I were well. Arguments with Rashawn continued and being home with him was worse than staying at the hospital. It got so bad at one point, I got myself dressed and decided I was going to drive myself back to the hospital so that I could get some rest. My children called my mother who convinced me not to go. She gave Rashawn and the children a lecture about the necessity for their assistance in my recovery.

After that incident, things got somewhat better. I found myself back at work quicker than the required six weeks.

Rashawn was not a provider despite the fact that he worked. Things were so bad financially I borrowed money from my sister just to maintain. It was an awful feeling knowing getting sick was not an option. If I couldn't function, the home would fall apart. I had to find strength when all seemingly obvious sources were depleted.

The remainder of our years together was much of the same. I was so miserable in this so-called marriage. My daughters were just as miserable and couldn't stand Rashawn. They only tolerated him for my sake.

I was exhausted by my own dysfunctional ways. Why did I walk down that aisle? I was absolutely driven by my need to appear to be something I was not. I didn't want people to see me as a failure, especially as it related to relationships. I once heard or read something somewhere that stated your partner is a mirror reflection of yourself. I didn't understand what that meant. I wasn't lazy or abusive or any of those things. Looking back, I now see that I was a lie, a huge facade; just like he was.

I had already disappointed myself so much. I had given in to this miserable life I had created. Divorce was out of the question. Once is bad enough, but twice was beyond my comprehension. I kept myself in denial, not wanting to face myself. I had done it again. I thought I had it all together and I was dead wrong.

I continued to attend church every Sunday. I don't know why I felt I needed to do this, but I did. I became extremely unfulfilled in my church. I yearned for more. I wanted someone, somewhere to give me some guidance, some direction. I wanted to hear something that would help me to understand this Bible, this book full of words, that made no sense to me.

All my life, I had heard that all of life's answers are in that book. I had heard how incredible this book was. I needed to know how God was supposed to help me. Could God help us?

VICTORIA A. ECKSTEIN

I proposed to Rashawn that we should start visiting different churches together. He found my church very boring and frankly, so did I. We began to visit different churches but nothing clicked.

His family had been involved in the church, but their faith seemed so foreign to me. They would do things that I wasn't familiar or comfortable with. They would pray out loud and openly praise God. This was totally uncomfortable to me. They openly spoke about God and the Bible. I always saw religion as a private experience.

At that time, I saw his family as hypocritical. They all seemed to justify Rashawn's behaviors. Didn't they realize how crazy he was? My kids and I always seemed to be the blame for everything that happened. What I didn't see was that his family only knew what he told them. He presented my daughters and I as the villains. He left them with the impression that I was money hungry and took all of his money. What money?

What they weren't aware of is that I carried all of the bills and all of the household expenses. Sure, on his payday, which was biweekly, he would initially hand me $300. Leaving $200 in his own pocket. He didn't pay child support and did nothing with this money except spend it on video games and comic books. Meanwhile, we barely had groceries.

To make matters worse, he wanted his sons to spend the weekend at the house all of the time. This was a major problem, because there was barely enough food in the house and no extra money to feed his two children all weekend. If he would have used some of that $200 worth of pocket money on food, it would have been no problem to have his children spend the weekend. But, it never happened. Instead, it was left for me to figure out.

I had a soft heart and felt bad for the children. I didn't want them to suffer as a result of their father's selfishness. I would often figure out a way to feed everyone all weekend with no money. I don't know how, but I did. I never took credit for this and let myself remain the villain.

The $300 he gave me towards expenses was immediately deposited into the joint checking account. His $300 along with my $1,000. The bills exceeded the money. I would write out checks to cover whatever bill I could. Little did I know, he was writing out checks to himself for the $300 he had contributed.

As a result of this act of selfishness, the checks I had written would bounce and fees would incur. Not only did I have to cover the bills, now I had to borrow money to cover expenses. He did this often and created deeper and deeper debt.

My career had changed by this time and I was no longer working as a court stenographer. I was now a certified batterer's intervention counselor. I also had a full-time job as a social worker.

During this marriage, I had completed my undergraduate degree in social work. I graduated with honors. I went to school on the weekends and worked a full-time job. It was hard taking care of a family and maintaining good grades in school and working full-time. In addition to all of this, I received my certification in running groups for perpetrators of domestic violence and did this part time.

I began to save my extra money from my part-time job running groups. I made decent money as a social worker. I changed the joint account to an individual account and managed all of the money matters. He resented this change in the account. It now meant any money he gave me for bills, he had no access to.

I started to explore how I could achieve home ownership. This had always been a dream of mine. Living in projects growing up, I never thought this could be a possibility for me. But, I wanted more for my children. I did not want them to grow up as I did. I was determined.

Eventually, Rashawn and I were approved for a loan to buy

a home with our combined incomes. I began to search for the perfect home and as a result found a home I fell in love with. The house was vacant and I looked into what this home would cost. There was no sign on the outside indicating it was for sale but something drew me to this house.

I discovered the house was a foreclosure with a special package attached to it. The bank would cover the closing costs and would pay for $4,000 worth of repairs on the home before closing. This was ideal. Ideal, except for one major problem. I did not feel right about buying a house with Rashawn. I didn't want him to have any part of this.

I put in a call to the mortgage company who had approved the loan. I told them that I did not want to buy the house with Rashawn and asked to re-figure the loan with just my income. I was told that it probably wouldn't happen with just my income because I did not make enough money.

I wanted this house so badly. I prayed about it and asked God what I should do. I kept having this nagging feeling inside directing me back to Proverbs 3:5 & 6. That is the same passage that instructed me to trust in the Lord and not rely on my own understanding. I repeated it over and over. Trying to fully absorb its meaning. I went to sleep with this scripture on my mind.

The next day, I had no anxiety about the situation with the house. I was ready to let it go. If it was in God's plan for me to own this home, it would happen. If it wasn't then it was probably for the best. I called the mortgage company and told them if I couldn't get the loan in my name alone, then the deal was off.

Next thing I knew, the mortgage company had told me they had reworked the figures and had figured out a way for me to own this home. Sure enough, God had blessed me with this home. It was such a huge blessing that I had obtained it with only $1,000 out of my pocket.

Once inside the house, it was apparent that the house needed some work. I could never get Rashawn to do anything around the house. I found myself painting rooms while he sat upstairs and watched television. I repaired things I didn't know how to repair, with no assistance. He never mowed the lawn or raked the leaves. There was 2.8 acres of land in the back of the house. He didn't even take out the trash. He did nothing. Everything that needed to be done, I did. This was in addition to working and maintaining the regular household chores, such as cooking and cleaning and taking care of the kid's needs.

There was a faucet in the basement that needed to be replaced. I begged him to get that faucet replaced many, many times. The water would just run out of the faucet. I didn't have the money to get it repaired and getting it from him was not even a consideration. Meanwhile, the water bill was getting out of control. This later turned out to be a problem bigger than I could have ever imagined. But, for now I was able to pay small portions of the massive bill.

As time went by, I began to suspect he had some type of drug problem. Cold medications with high alcohol content would disappear. My daughters reported seeing him in the backyard smoking something. He would come in the house reeking of the smell of marijuana. When confronted, he would lie and make up things about the girls.

He constantly competed with them for my attention. It felt like I had three children, instead of two. He would tell big stories about the girls to get them in trouble with me or create some kind of controversy to divert my attention away from him. Not only that, he did it to be spiteful.

I began to find drug paraphernalia hidden in the house. What I found indicated he may be smoking crack cocaine. I confronted him about this and it led to a huge argument. Once again, he lunged at me, knocking me on the bed with his hands around my throat. He began to choke me. I pushed him hard as

I could with a look of sheer terror on my face. He immediately let go of my neck with a look of fright on his face. He seemed to be shocked at himself, not thinking he would do this again. He begged me not to call the police. So, I didn't.

Instead, I began to plan how and when I would get out of this. It took awhile before the right moment made itself available but it finally came. As usual, we were having a heated argument and he began to threaten me as I walked away from him. I told him the girls had been instructed to call the police. I told him I would have the police remove him from my home if he threatened me one more time. I gave him one hour to get his things together and to get out of my home on his own. I told him I planned to file for divorce.

He did not like this one bit and said something that I will never forget. He replied, "Go ahead, get your divorce. While you're at it, go raise those two b------ you never raised!" That was it!!!! I marched upstairs and told him he now had 20 minutes and I never wanted to see or hear from him again. I told him I was taking a short nap and did not care to see his face when I woke up.

He began packing his bags and slamming things around. I gave him one last instruction about not banging things around. I lay down on the bed and prayed quietly. I asked God to keep me safe and to let this nightmare finally end. I fell asleep with a sense of peace. When I awoke, he was gone.

The kids and I celebrated his departure. I had all of the locks changed immediately and was ready to do things differently.

I saw my addiction to toxic relationships as that of an addiction to coffee loaded with artificial sweeteners. The taste is bittersweet. The sweetness of the coffee is not the real thing but a cheap imitation. The taste of the coffee itself is something I didn't really like, but somehow I felt compelled to ingest it. It was addictive and I was drawn to it daily to keep me going throughout the day.

I made up my mind that I was giving up coffee and would look into the possibility of tea. It was soothing and comforting and didn't have to have sweeteners to make it taste good. The sugar just complimented it.

Chapter Eight

Spiritual Awakening

PRIOR TO THE END of our marriage, Rashawn and I continued seeking out a church that we might be able to belong to and attend together. In the process, we learned Rashawn's mother had changed her membership from the church she had been loyal to for years. She found her new church home helpful in her life and felt it may assist Rashawn and I in our marriage.

The pastor of this church was young, energetic and dynamic. The talk around town was that he brought forth a powerful sermon. My aunt had also been a member for years and encouraged me to give this church at try. Rashawn, of course, pushed me to try this church because his mother had become a member.

I wasn't very open to the idea. It was rumored that some of the women in the church sought to make this pastor their husband. He was engaged to a beautiful woman and I was appalled to hear about this type of behavior among church members.

After much hesitation, I decided to give it a try. Besides, what could it hurt? Rashawn and I went together. I left church stunned. This experience proved itself to be so powerful, wonderful, and unique, I wanted to come back. The pastor was an educated man with a dynamic presentation. His approach didn't resort to hootin' and hollerin' about nothing. Instead, he taught you, he educated you on how to have a better life. He would go directly into the Bible and reveal the meaning of scriptures and parables and apply them to everyday life situations. It was obvious he was blessed with the anointing of God on his life. His age provided him with the ability to relate to both young and old alike. He had a unique way of talking about real life issues and delivered guidance as to how to straighten out your life.

Rashawn's discomfort was visible during the sermon. The sermon could have been directly spoken to Rashawn as opposed to the entire congregation. I loved it. I knew it was unpleasant for him and was touching every nerve in his body. He twitched and fidgeted so much, I thought he was having an allergic reaction to something.

The sermon plainly talked about a man's role within the home. It lent itself as a guide for families toward healing. It provided answer for correcting troubled marriages. I realized God was the answer for us. The sermon stirred up unspoken realities for Rashawn. He knew he wasn't the ideal husband or stepfather. What it did for me was totally different. It brought forth a small glimmer of light into the darkness in which I dwelled. I didn't deserve to live the way I lived.

Inside I struggled with leaving the church I had always belonged to versus becoming a member of this church that was feeding me with useful information as to how to change my life. I felt a strong sense of loyalty to the Catholic church. This had been the only church I had really known. I didn't know what to do. I felt alive in this new church and could hardly wait for Sunday to come. Soon, I would make up my mind.

It was Mother's Day and, as usual, I was miserable at home. I escaped my unfulfilled life at home and ran to my source of restoration. The pastor preached a sermon that totally touched every fiber of my being. He spoke about women like me. He talked about the struggles of being a mother and especially targeted single mothers. He went on to say that you could be married and still functioning as a single mother. That was me! How did he know?

He referred to a story in the Bible involving two women. One woman, Sarai, could not bear children. Sarai was the wife of Abram. God had promised Abram that he would become the father of a great nation. He further told Abram that he would become famous and a huge blessing to others. God sent Abram out of the country he had been familiar with to an unfamiliar region. Abram had to leave his home in order to receive the promises of God. This required a great act of faith. God told him to settle in this land and that he would give this land to Abram's offspring.

At that time, Abram was a 75-year-old man. Abram did as God instructed him to do. As time passed, Abram asked God about his promise for a son. Abram even questioned God asking how can he be sure this will happen for him. God once again reassured him of his promise.

Ten years later, Sarai became impatient with God. When the promise wasn't fulfilled quick enough, this woman took it upon herself to ask her husband to impregnate one of the servants, Hagar.

Her husband went along with her plan and slept with Hagar. Hagar did indeed become pregnant. When Hagar learned of her pregnancy, she began to treat Sarai with contempt. Sarai got mad at Abram, blaming Hagar's anger on Abram. Sarai told Abram that God would deal with him for what was happening with Hagar.

Abram told Sarai that she could deal with Hagar herself. Sarai began to treat Hagar badly, causing Hagar to run away. An angel found Hagar and told her to return to Sarai and submit to her authority. The angel then made a promise to Hagar.

Hagar would have more descendants than she could count. The angel further instructed her to name her unborn son, Ishmael, which means God hears. The angel told Hagar that her son would be wild and unpopular.

Hagar did as the angel instructed her and her son was born. Abram named the child Ishmael as the angel prophesized. God then told Abram he was going to bless him in a great way. He changed his name to Abraham, which means father of many nations. God also changed Sarai's name to Sarah, which means princess. He then told Abraham he would bless Sarah and give her a son.

Abraham laughed to himself. He was now 100 years old. He questioned how he was to become a father at his age. Sarah was now 90. Abraham thought God was speaking of Ishmael. But God told him his wife would have a son. He was to name him Isaac, which means he laughs. Sarah also laughed at God's promise to Abraham.

It was her feeling that God had missed His time to bless her. God confronted her about her lack of faith. Sarah denied laughing. She lied to God. God quickly told her that he knew she was lying. He knew she laughed. He wanted her to know He had heard her.

Lo and behold, God had fulfilled his promise. Sarah became pregnant and gave birth to Isaac in her old age. Now there were two sons born of this husband, one of his wife and one of his servant. Sarah wanted no parts of the servant and her child. Sarah did not want Ishmael sharing in the family inheritance with her son, Isaac. She told Abraham to send Hagar and Ishmael away.

Abraham was very upset because Ishmael was his son. Abraham turned to God and God told him to do what Sarah asked of him. God told Abraham Ishmael's descendents would make a great nation. The next morning Abraham sent Hagar and Ishmael into the wilderness with minimal provisions. The woman was sent off to care for her child, alone. She was a single parent.

Eventually the food and water ran out. Hagar had been wandering aimlessly in the wilderness with her child. She had no means to provide for her child and did not know what to do. She called on God for help. God heard the cries of her son and told Hagar not to worry. He had a plan for Ishmael. His descendents would be great. God immediately opened Hagar's eyes and she saw a well that God had provided. Hagar and Ishmael remained in the wilderness where Ishmael became an expert archer.

The pastor preached about being born into the worst of circumstances just as Ishmael was. He further elaborated where you come from does not determine your outcome in life. He pointed out what can happen when we decide we can't wait on God. The story shows you what can happen when we decide to take matters into our own hands. Utter confusion and disorder resulted in the choices of Sarah. This was compared to the choices we make in our own lives. He spoke about the abandonment of single mothers by the child's father and the hurt and pain it creates in our lives.

The pastor then compared this story to real life circumstances. He paralleled God's moving Abram out of familiar land with people having to move from where they are in life to another realm in order to receive God's blessing. This is a huge feat for anyone and could be very uncomfortable. But you have to begin to walk in the spirit (which dwells inside) and out of the flesh to position yourself for God. It takes a tremendous amount of faith to move from your familiar way of living life to a new, uncommon way of living. Pastor spoke about Hagar and Ishmael surviving in the wilderness. He talked about single mothers going through hard times, feeling lost and lonely and struggling to survive in the wilderness. He pointed out Ishmael's accomplishment while in the wilderness. He not only survived but he became an expert in the field of archery. He spoke about being molded and shaped in the midst of what seems to be the worst of life's circumstances.

God had a plan for Ishmael. He had a purpose. He fulfilled his promises to both Sarah and Hagar. The sermon was such an inspiration, I decided to join this church. I never realized the Bible contained so much drama. It was refreshing to learn people have endured the same type of pain, the same heartache and made the same bad choices even back then.

I began to attend church services consistently every Sunday along with Bible study classes during the week. I tried desperately to convince Rashawn to commit to saving this awful marriage. I pointed out reliance on God for direction couldn't be bad. How could we go wrong? I emphasized this needed to be a joint venture. He wanted no part of it. Rashawn would not continue to go.

Regardless of what Rashawn wanted, I had decided I wanted to become a part of this. I started to achieve insight, direction and strength. As I grew more diligent in my faith, the situation at home began to look differently. God was gently steering my path towards healing. The road ahead of me was long. Flushing out the negativity imbedded in my thoughts presented as a cumbersome task. The first area to target was my marriage.

I questioned whether or not I had gone ahead of God's plan and created this so-called marriage, as opposed to waiting on God to deliver my divine partner. I felt pressure mounting to make this marriage work. I decided to make an appointment to speak with this pastor one-on-one. I had built up such anxiety about this meeting, I began to get nervous twitches in my eye. I was ashamed of my life and felt so much like "the sinner." I knew I had to be honest about everything if I was really going to get the help I needed.

Unexpectedly, the pastor was inviting and down-to-earth. I spoke to him from my heart about the complexities of my situation. Not knowing what to expect, anticipating a therapy session, I walked away feeling I was speaking to a trusted friend who passed no judgment. We spoke like old friends. At the time, pastor was engaged to his now wife. He spoke about his love for his fiancée and his eagerness to make her his bride.

I found it endearing. It warmed my heart to hear a man speak so beautifully about the woman he loved. He offered spiritual direction and opened my eyes to the beauty of love and its potential for goodness. The Bible served as the only source of his derived wisdom. I saw the biblical stance on marital relationships and what they are supposed to look like.

Clearly, it looked nothing like mine. I had to get out of this mess. I just didn't know how or when. I tapped into my newly formed relationship with God. I sought his wisdom through prayer. Finally, the day came when I knew what to do.

I learned marriage involves a union between two people. The union must be blessed by God. My marriage had nothing to do with God or his blessing. It stemmed from my own inability to wait on God as well as my longing for immediate gratification. I discovered a loving God will protect us from making a mistake, if only we would listen to Him. If we go ahead of God, then we have to resign ourselves to deal with the consequences of our decisions. I had really felt the consequences of my bad choices. I wanted a different life and I did not want to make poor choices in my relationships. I wanted to be sure I had really learned the lesson this time. Time would be the true indicator of my success.

It's one thing to have the tools you need to begin to repair. It's an entirely different thing to know how to use the tools effectively in order to fix what is broken. You have to begin to work with the tools in order to determine how they work. Had I mastered this repair job or was I just collecting the tools necessary for the project and discovering its intended use?

Chapter Nine

In the Beginning

JEROME AND I MET approximately three and a half years ago. My second divorce became finalized less than a year prior. I was reeling from this ordeal emotionally. I had lost a significant amount of weight and my eyes reflected the numbness of my feelings. Stress seemed to be my closest ally.

In addition to working a full-time job, I also entertained myself by attending graduate school on a full-time basis on the weekends. I worked a part-time internship as a school adjustment counselor and continued to run intervention groups for the perpetrators of domestic violence. Living in the home were my daughters, Monique and Nicole, myself and my granddaughter, Farrah (the light of my life). Monique experienced an extremely trying pregnancy. She had gone into premature labor three months prior to her due date. She became hospitalized as a result of her early labor. She developed gestational diabetes and carried an extremely high white blood cell count. I provided both the financial and emotional support for her throughout this ordeal. Fortunately, she delivered a beautiful, healthy baby girl two months early. The baby was not underweight.

Finances were disastrous and I was in danger of losing the

home I had worked so hard to obtain. I was sinking in a sea of muck. Unfortunately, the unrepaired water faucet had created a bill so large, I could no longer afford to keep up with it. As a result of Rashawn's neglect, this huge bill became attached to the taxes owed on my home. This raised my mortgage payment to an additional $500 a month increase in payments. I was struggling and looked everywhere I could for help. There was none. It was only a matter of time before I lost everything I worked so hard to accomplish.

I had no time to breathe and no moment to focus on me. My children were pretty much running the house. As a matter of fact, they were pretty much running me. My life was in utter upheaval and I desperately wanted control over my life. I was falling fast!

Life, at that time, involved more of "going through the motions" than anything else. I couldn't find stillness long enough to enjoy it. My day began at the crack of dawn and went into the late evening hours. There were days when I would eat nothing for the entire day. I functioned on pure adrenaline. If I had attained a quiet moment, I would wrestle with its benefits. I couldn't sit still long enough to enjoy it. I would constantly create movement or busy myself. I was a wreck. Fortunately, the church seemed to provide some answers for my crazy life's dilemmas.

My dysfunction manifested itself in my adult life in several different ways. There are many addictions in this world and I believe, at that time, I was addicted to chaos and drama. It felt normal and comforting to me. When things went smoothly, I didn't function well and was extremely restless.

I met Jerome in the lobby of an office building I had been working in. As I entered the lobby from the corner store, I spotted Jerome. I remembered him from several years ago. He was working through an agency whose office was in the same building.

We made small talk and went on our way. After three or four encounters on the elevator, he asked me if I would like to go to lunch. I thought it was a harmless gesture and decided lunch would be okay. Following lunch, we spoke on the telephone quite often. Our relationship developed very slowly. We were friends for several months before the relationship moved to another level.

Jerome is a handsome man with the physique of a body builder. His smile is winning and his personality pleasant. His friendship was refreshing. Pressure was nonexistent.

Conversations centered around our desire to serve God and to live a Christian lifestyle. I had already been involved in the church for a little more than a year and had started implementing changes. I had begun an incredible healing process but had such a long journey ahead of me. I found the answer for my life and had decided to stay on the path of this long journey.

Jerome also was working on a major healing process. He shared bits and pieces of his life and the prior lifestyle he had lived. He came back to Massachusetts from Georgia where he had been residing for the last eight years. He had several family members in the area and missed their visible presence in his life. He had six sisters, five of which were living in the area. His mother also lived in the area. He was living with her temporarily.

In Atlanta, he had gotten into a major accident and came close to losing his life. This, along with his sister's illness, brought him back to the area to be closer to family.

Jerome quickly became aware of my financial situation and my disorderly life. My persistence in seeking assistance was running thin. I received no assistance from anywhere or anybody except Jerome. Jerome felt it important he help me out of my current financial problems. I spoke to him several times about not wanting to be obligated to anyone. I told him not to spend any of his hard-earned money on my property. I could not afford to pay him back.

Jerome did not value money that way. He viewed money as a God-given blessing. He told me I was an incredible, hard-working woman and that he hated to see any woman struggle. He often said he wasn't really sure why he needed to help me but he felt he had to.

Jerome not only provided money to allow me to keep my home, he also hired contractors to come and do repair work on the home at no charge to myself. It disturbed him greatly that my former husband never helped around the house and allowed things to deteriorate.

I began to feel I was being blessed. In return for Jerome's help, I became creative in helping him. I would cook him a warm meal or provide him transportation to and from work. He would never accept any type of financial return on my part. My goal was to show him that I was not money hungry and did not care for him, because of his generosity.

Our friendship grew stronger over time. We would attend church services together from time to time and attend family and social events. This relationship was very fulfilling for me. I had no commitments in anyway. Apparently, I was appreciated for who I was.

This was strange and new for me. Other relationships I had entertained or had been committed to, never involved God. Friendship usually came after the fact, if at all. Jerome would shower me with gifts and tend to my every need.

It felt like a dream come true. I started to develop feelings for him outside of the friendship. I wanted to proceed with caution. Jerome was a man who had no children, had never been engaged and had never even lived with a woman. Issues from his past (the ones he revealed), presented as a thing of the past.

I disclosed my prior trauma and history of abuse. He told me of abuse and trauma he witnessed and was exposed to as a child. I noticed he struggled with issues of trust and was very guarded. It seemed somewhat strange but I understood. I also had my guard up, but nowhere near the extent of his apparent fears.

It was hard to get a feel for him. If we were sitting on a couch together and my arm accidentally brushed up against his, he would nearly jump off of the couch. He seemed perfectly content with just being in my presence. He often commented about his comfort level in my home. He said he felt, in spite of the chaos, the atmosphere was saturated with God's presence.

He would often come over to watch television or talk for a while. His comfort level was very apparent. I found it strange that a man so guarded would find comfort in my home and in my presence. At times, he would fall asleep on the couch and stay all night. His sleep seemed to be much needed. He seemed restless within his own skin and my home seemed to be a source of comfort and peace for him.

Our conversations were rich and intelligent. I knew this man had a higher calling on his life. We studied the Bible together and spoke about God. It felt like I had my own personal preacher. We would discuss something relative to the wonderful workings of God and the next day the same sermon would be spoken by another preacher. If it wasn't a preacher on television that was highly respected, it was from a minister at a church. This man knew the word of God.

The night came when our relationship would change forever. It was a day like any other. Jerome had called several times that day. I had not been home the majority of the day and had missed all of his calls. I finally connected with him in the early evening hours. We had a brief conversation, and he asked if he could come over later. I told him that would be fine, provided it wasn't too late. He said he would call back in about an hour as he had been watching a football game at a friend's house.

An hour later, he called as promised, stating he would be over in about two hours when the game ended. No problem. I was busy studying anyway. Two hours passed and he called once again stating he would be over shortly. An hour passed and he hadn't shown up. I started to get upset but figured he would be here shortly.

Another twenty minutes had passed and he called again. He apologized for not being here but stated it was really important he speak with me. I told him not to bother coming over and I would see him tomorrow. He insisted I wait for him because he really had something he wanted to discuss with me that couldn't wait.

I was intrigued by the importance of this conversation. More time had passed, and no Jerome. Finally, my doorbell rang. My children were asleep and it was late. I opened the door and it was Jerome standing there looking somewhat out of sorts.

I asked him if he was all right. He told me he was. He seemed to be slightly intoxicated. I asked him if he had been drinking and he honestly stated he had. Slightly irritated, I asked him what he needed to talk to me about.

He started his speech with the skill of a preadolescent. He stated, "Vic, you know I like you a lot, right?"

I responded, "I guess so."

Before I knew it, he replied, "Hell, Vic, I love you." He went on further to say he loved everything about me and was confused about his feelings. He didn't know what to do with all of that love. He wanted to become a couple and to take our friendship to another level. He adamantly stated this had nothing to do with trying to get sex. He and I had not been intimate in anyway.

I looked at him with a slight grin. It found it somewhat cute and enlightening to see someone struggle so hard to tell me he loved me. I quickly dismissed this conversation and figured he would sleep it off and forget about it in the morning. He seemed so relieved to get those words out. I thought about his confession a little longer and marveled at how he spent all day developing the courage to tell me something so simple.

We spent the rest of the evening in each other's arms in a candle lit room with soft music playing. We talked for a little while and eventually fell asleep. I dismissed the entire situation and assumed this situation would look differently in the morning. Besides, I was just fine with our friendship. The thought of things changing in anyway produced some anxiety about what that might look like. I decided to enjoy the moment.

Upon waking in the morning, Jerome arose from the couch with a pleasant "Good morning," I responded in kind. Convinced he had forgotten last night, I asked him how he was feeling. He told me he was just fine. Perplexed, I asked him if he remembered anything about last night.

Surprisingly, he had remembered every detail of everything that was said or occurred. He reiterated his feelings and his desire to begin this relationship. I decided at this point, I would give this relationship a try. I told him I loved him as well and was happy about our decision to become a couple.

Our newfound relationship continued to stay as pleasing as our friendship. Jerome had begun to assist in sorting out my home life and bring a sense of order into my environment. He provided increased spiritual guidance. My children were resistant to this house cleaning venture and resented this new man in my life.

I definitely understood their feelings, considering all they had been through with Rashawn. I felt torn. It was time for change and I invited the changes where I saw fit. From my children's perception, I was being controlled by Jerome.

Jerome never gave advice without pointing out how it could help either myself or my children become better people. I was aware of my constant appeasing of my children and catering to their every need and whim. It was draining and not beneficial

111

for them. I began to implement changes and am truly grateful I did.

I watched Monique, a mother herself, obtain a sense of independence. She had been sent out of the nest to fly. She had outgrown the comfort of the nest but had great fear about life outside of it. It was the hardest thing in the world for this mother to do. I knew it had to be done. Fortunately, my baby bird eventually soared with the strength of an eagle.

Over time, things got better and everyone adjusted to each other. As Jerome and I became more familiar with each other, I began to notice areas of concern. He started purchasing items that seemed a bit pricey. This happened much too frequently for my comfort. I inquired as to the source of this money. I didn't feel right about these gifts and wondered where they were coming from.

He confessed he had done some illegal things in his past and had actually served time in jail for this in Atlanta. He told me it was relative to credit card fraud. He adamantly denied being involved with this anymore and stated all of the gifts he provided were legitimate. I requested copies of both his paystub and his police record. He provided both.

This eased my discomfort somewhat. I insisted he stop buying so many items. I wanted a receipt for anything he brought into my home. I've never knowingly accepted illegal money and would not start now. Jerome began to discover he did not need to keep me by providing for me. All he needed to do was to be himself. I wanted him to know that I loved him and not what he could do for me.

Knowing this, gave him great comfort. He told me he had never met a woman that loved him that way. In Atlanta, he encountered many women who wanted to be with him because of his kindness and giving ways. He found our relationship to be quite refreshing.

Jerome began to miss Atlanta and decided to take a vacation

for a week to visit. He had several friends whom he missed. I encouraged his trip and wanted him to enjoy himself. The first week without him hadn't been too difficult. I knew he was coming back and I was happy he had an opportunity to enjoy himself.

My schedule would not permit me to go anywhere. I had too many obligations and commitments to tend to. I was actually too busy to notice. Jerome's one-week vacation, turned into a two weeks and then three. Confusion crept in. He called constantly, telling me how much he missed me and how badly he wanted to be back. Yet, he continually prolonged this trip.

He eventually told me he had some things he had to tie up and was tending to some personal matters. He wasn't very forthcoming about what it was he had to do, but I didn't feel a great sense of concern. Simultaneously, I had been getting information from his best friend who had informed me that Jerome told him he had no intentions of coming back.

I confronted Jerome about this and he told me it wasn't true. The third week turned into a fourth week. I decided I was not going to tolerate this anymore and demanded some answers. I wasn't going to put my life on hold for him or anybody else. If he wasn't coming back that would be fine. I just wanted to know. He immediately let me know he had booked his flight and would be back in two days.

I met him at the airport and was glad to see him. He presented me with a gift that he had purchased in Atlanta. I opened the box he handed me and was shocked to see the most beautiful bracelet I had ever been given. It was white gold with several diamonds. The shape of the bracelet was unique. I felt special. It appeared to be very expensive.

Jerome said he had every intention of coming back but he had some fines and penalties that needed clearing up in Atlanta. He had been on probation for his credit card fraud conviction and had to pay restitution for items received. Jerome stated he wanted to get all aspects of his life in order and did not want to carry any baggage into this relationship.

He stated it was an embarrassment for him and he was ashamed of what he had done. He went to Atlanta to resolve it but it took longer than he anticipated. Paperwork had been lost and he needed documentation to present to his probation officer in Massachusetts. I respected him for handling this situation on his own.

Jerome eventually moved into my home and implemented a budget that allowed for paying bills, home repairs and saving money. He kept up the property and the aesthetics of the house.

As time went by, a darker side of Jerome was beginning to emerge. The first area of concern began with his going out with his friends and coming home at unacceptable hours. I didn't mind him spending time with his friends on occasion. I did mind him coming in at unreasonable hours. It began to happen on a frequent basis and eventually led to him getting kicked out of the house and sent back to his mother's house.

Jerome explained he had lived the fast life in Atlanta for so many years and sometimes it was hard for him to adjust to his new lifestyle with me. Partying and spending time at strip clubs was his norm. In Atlanta, strip clubs and bars were everywhere. It was no big deal for him.

He reminded me that he had been a single male for so long and was used to doing whatever he wanted, whenever he wanted. He stated he was trying his best to adjust but at times it got hard. I told him I did not want a man in my life who hung out in bars and strip clubs. I was trying to live a Christian lifestyle and I thought this was his goal as well.

He reassured me that it was his goal. He pointed out areas of weakness that existed in me. He reminded me that just because I had a struggle or a weak area didn't mean I didn't want to serve God. It sounded like a valid point and I decided to give things another chance.

As time went by, Jerome's one chance turned into many chances. Jerome would be the perfect partner for periods of three to six months. During those wonderful months, I became lulled into the notion that things are really going to be different this time. The good times were the best. I didn't want to give that up.

I would find myself justifying the bad situations by telling myself he was only hurting himself. I didn't want to recognize the impact it was having on myself and my daughter.

There have been so many instances with Jerome, they are too numerous to count. There have been nights where he never came home. There have been instances where I questioned whether or not he has brought other women into my house. There have been explosions of anger and rage. He ruined the one and only vacation I have ever had in my life. He has gotten high and intoxicated after hanging out all night.

In combination with that, there have been times when I have been treated like the queen of the castle. I never had to ask for anything and all of my needs were taken care of. The house was always kept up and Jerome would cook surprise meals or do the grocery shopping. He took great care of the house and made sure there was always money to pay the bills. If I had an ache or a pain, he would ensure I got my proper rest. He took care of me when I was sick and tried to keep me happy when I was well. I never had to fish for compliments. He always made me feel beautiful.

Jerome could be the sweetest, most gentle person on the planet when he wasn't under the influence of something. But when he was, he was a nightmare. Being with him was always confusing. Just when I thought I had enough, he would do something incredibly wonderful that would suck me back in.

Life with him was similar to being caught in a maze. It was full of twists and turns. There would be times when I would feel I was on the right path and just when I would feel good

VICTORIA A. ECKSTEIN

about where I was going, I would get hit with another wall. It was so unbelievably hard to let go of. As time passed, his behaviors and patterns seemed to be revealing themselves less frequently.

A year prior, we had arranged to be married. One month before its scheduled date, I decided to cancel it. There was no burning desire to get married (which was a first for me) and intuition was telling me it wasn't a good idea at that time. Now, due to the significant improvement in our partnership, it was a good time to commit to each other.

We were once again preparing for marriage. It was our belief that God would not look favorably upon our living arrangements. Jerome and I did not share an intimate relationship. We were trying to save ourselves for marriage. I had been married twice already and he had never been married. We wanted something special for our wedding day and were willing to sacrifice sex. Besides, we wanted God's blessing for this union.

I struggled at times with this life of celibacy, living in the same household, sharing the same bed. Had God been protecting me from something?

Nevertheless, it was my belief that he was finally mastering his coping skills and was on the path to leading a life full of promise. Our friendship was strong and our love for each other was true. We hadn't had any issues for a long period of time. We both shared our goals and dreams for our marriage. I had reservations but hoped this was a good time to solidify this union. That is, until I picked up the telephone and heard his voice saying…

Chapter Ten

Hallelujah Anyhow

RAPE! I WAS SHOCKED. I couldn't believe what I was hearing. My ears heard him but my inner being couldn't fully comprehend the entire message delivered. I sat down for a minute and tried to determine what to do next. What would I tell Nicole?

I functioned through the morning in full denial of what I heard. Everything seemed foggy and surreal. I moved through my usual routine as if nothing had happened. Then the telephone calls began.

His mother called and asked if I would go to the police station with her because Jerome needed some clothing. I did not want to go. She sounded as upset and confused as I was. I decided to go with her. I was in a fog and a daze. We were given minimal information at the police station.

An officer spoke with us briefly and told us Jerome had been arrested for rape, kidnapping, resisting arrest and assault and battery. We left the station just as confused. Neither one of us could believe he had done anything remotely close to rape. We both agreed he had issues but saw no indications of his capability in inflicting cruelty of this nature and magnitude.

Once home, I sat quietly. I was still in a state of shock. I sat on the edge of the couch, staring into space. The phone rang and abruptly shook me out of my daze. My mother was on the line hysterical. She just saw Jerome on the news. I became hysterical and began crying uncontrollably. This is the first time the reality of the situation actually hit me.

My phone then rang several times. Each caller had a different version of the news report. My ears were flooded with a variety of conversations. Everyone had something to tell me. Everyone had speculations about whether he did it or not. I felt overwhelmed and was drowning in a sea of bewilderment.

Sleep never came that night and many nights following. My overwrought brain wouldn't permit my attendance at work. I gave myself a day to recoup. I went to work the following day and was greeted with the same sea of confusion. I was bombarded by coworkers who had seen the news and wanted to know details. I couldn't focus on my work and decided to leave early.

Once I arrived home, I retrieved a voice mail message from my church pastor. He called to express his concern. He saw the article in the newspaper regarding Jerome. He left several numbers for me to contact him. I called him back and welcomed his support. I found myself saying things I normally would not have said.

I told the pastor I was having a really hard time but knew God was my source. I told him I would be okay. He passed no judgment and wanted to make sure Nicole and I were fine. I alleviated his concerns and expressed appreciation for his call. Our conversation, although short in duration, offered lasting comfort. Not because of anything particular said. Just because the pastor took the time to call.

The next day at work, I struggled to get through the day. I performed my job to the best of my ability. I decided I needed to speak with someone at the church. I needed a word from God. I went to the church and spoke to the assistant pastor.

I waited downstairs in the church office until she was ready to meet with me. Once summoned up to her office, I walked into the room and she immediately hugged me. She told me she knew why I was there and had been praying prior to letting me upstairs, seeking answers for what exactly she should say to me during this crisis situation.

The pastor told me that the only thing she can say to me is, "Stand by your man." Stand by your man? What in the world was she talking about? This man had been accused of raping someone. The assistant pastor continued to tell me that she does not believe Jerome had raped anyone and that the truth of the entire situation would reveal itself in the end. She further stated whatever I decided to do was my decision, but her spirit is telling her that Jerome did not rape anyone. She asked me if I had spoken to Jerome. I told her I had not. She told me to hear what he has to say before I make any decisions. I decided to listen to her. I left her feeling indecisive yet stronger.

I would go to see Jerome in jail the first opportunity I had. I needed to talk to him to get some answers. My first visit with him was the most difficult one. I felt embarrassed and ashamed. I didn't want anyone to notice me and I had no pride in this visit.

Our first visit was filled with tears and anguish. Jerome told me that he absolutely did not rape anyone. His lawyer had instructed him not to speak about the case. I knew this had been true because the lawyer had informed myself and his family members of her instructions outside of court. I left that visit not knowing anything about that night except what had been printed in the paper and splashed on the television screen.

With each passage of time, my perception of reality developed into a blur. The telephone constantly rang with an assortment of stories about Jerome. I received telephone calls from total strangers. People were saying cruel and nasty things about my, "rapist fiancé." Several unknown individuals came to my door seeking Jerome.

Court appearances were confusing as well. The prosecutor recited the specifics of the alleged crime in open court. On the night in question, a woman alleged she had been approached by Jerome in the early morning hours. Supposedly, he had propositioned the woman for sex and that she turned him down. She then alleges he grabbed her by the hair and dragged her up the street to an abandoned building. She further alleges he told her he had a gun and would kill her if she screamed. It was further alleged that he punched her in the face twice and proceeded to force himself upon her. Following the rape she states he left the building and she stayed behind in the building for a long period of time.

Then she states she got dressed and left the building, flagging down a motorist passing by. The motorist took her to the police station where she states Jerome was in front of the police station using the telephone. Jerome then left the scene and the police eventually found him and arrested him. The victim identified Jerome by an identifiable scar on his back.

The defense attorney stated this woman had admitted to using crack cocaine that night and had been drinking as well. The police report confirmed there were high levels of drugs and alcohol in her system. The defense attorney went on to talk about our wedding that was to take place in three weeks and asked the judge if he could be released in order to get married. The attorney emphasized Jerome's denial of raping anyone and spoke about his good job. The judge would not release Jerome but did allow a bail of $5,000 cash. I was shocked! What in the world was he thinking about? Marriage? I couldn't believe it.

My mind had really become a maze of twists and turns, with no clear direction. Thoughts were flooding my mind— "stand by your man," "identifiable scar," "I didn't do it," "it probably was consensual sex gone bad," etc. Everyone had an opinion. Everyone knew what I should do. Everyone except me.

Once again, I ran to the place that has provided me with much comfort and clear direction. I ran straight to the church. This was the week for revival and a guest preacher was to attend. This was the first night for the revival. I walked into the church, with many eyes on me. I knew people were aware of the situation and I felt so ashamed.

Unfortunately, cruelty can occur even in a church setting. Several people were comforting, and nonjudgmental. Others made inappropriate statements every opportunity they could get. It was hard for me to be there. I felt compelled to stay there and not run out of the door. There was a reason for my being there, I just hadn't discovered what it was yet.

I sat down next to my mother. My mother told me not to look so sad. I couldn't help it. I felt awful. I couldn't put on a face of strength, not this time. I wanted to feel the sadness and was wallowing in it. I couldn't eat. I couldn't sleep. My poor body was exhausted. My mind was mush.

As the guest preacher approached the pulpit, I noticed how small and fragile she appeared. She was small in stature and was dressed in a well-pressed suit with a white collared shirt. Her hair was swept up in a French twist and I didn't know quite what to expect. She looked like a nun in a suit.

I thought of that old saying, "Never judge a book by its cover." Okay, maybe she had something to say. As this small woman began to preach her sermon, the tears began to flow from my eyes. This woman, this preacher, began to preach the words *"Hallelujah Anyhow."* This phrase was a familiar phrase. I had sung it in the words of a song. I had heard it preached in a sermon. This phrase was something I knew in my head but had not planted firmly in my heart, my spirit, my soul.

Hallelujah Anyhow. What really is this simple phrase saying? Hallelujah is the highest form of praise you can give to God. Her message simply was to praise God for not only what he has done for you, not for what he's going to do for you in the future; but to praise Him in the middle of your hardship, your trial, your storm. She talked about trials and suffering as a normal process of life. She talked about going through the process and learning something while in the middle of it. Praise him even if you have no understanding of what is going to happen in your life.

I began to think about my life and realized prospective is in retrospect. Looking back over my life, I could visibly see how God saved me from death. He saved my life not once, but several times. He kept me strong in the midst of incredible battles. Through all of my trauma and heartaches, I have never experienced a nervous breakdown and have never been on any medication to treat any mental health issues. I have never had a substance abuse problem. God has remained my source, my therapist, my savior.

In every situation, every relationship, God's ultimate plan came to be. No matter how hard I tried to hang in there or try to make it right or make it better, I could not change what God has already destined to be. All I could ultimately do is to release it to God.

God has a unique, individual destiny for all of us. My struggle will not be your struggle. My trial will not be your trial. God knows what you can and cannot bear. The length of time it takes for us to arrive at our divine purpose in life, depends on how many times we divert off of the path God had mapped out for us to follow.

Once again, God had intervened in my life. What appeared to be a disaster was actually a blessing in disguise. It was disguised by its controversial nature. God stopped this marriage from taking place on two separate occasions. As the Bible so eloquently states, "There is a time for everything." Things happen in God's time, not ours. There were still unresolved issues that needed to be addressed before any marriage could be considered.

I thought about that scripture I hold so dear to my heart, Proverbs 3:5. Was I really trusting God with all of my heart? Or was I depending on my understanding of the situation? Could I let go and let God do whatever he has willed to do in my life? My soul was shaken up by the words coming out of this woman. It felt as if this sermon was tailored directly for my current situation. Once I allowed the anointed word of God being delivered through the words of this preacher into my soul, I felt a huge release of a mighty burden.

I lifted my head from its drooping position on my chest. I raised my head high and began to thank God and praise him for loving me so much. I thanked him for whatever he was doing or going to do for me in my life.

After I left church that evening, I felt a renewed sense of strength. My first impulse was to pray that God would make it all better. But I realized I needed to trust God and pray for his shaping and molding for my divine purpose in life. As opposed to praying for instant answers to my problem, I prayed for what I needed despite my lack of understanding of what was going on. I discovered I didn't have to have all of the answers as it related to this situation. Instead, I sought direction from God on how to react to what was happening despite the many unanswered questions. I realized I may never have all of the answers as to what happened on that night and I had to fully surrender myself and place all of my trust in God.

I needed to be strong. I went back to the jail on several occasions. Each time a different picture of the events began to emerge. Jerome told me that night he had been out hanging in the clubs and had left the downtown area, heading back home. He states he was approached by a woman and two men. He says he was a target of an attempted robbery. The men had used the woman to entice potential victims. Realizing this wasn't working in this situation, the men attempted to attack him. Jerome states he had gotten into a fight with these two men and had hurt one of them really badly. He stated he had hurt the man so badly that he was afraid he had hurt him. Because of his fear, he headed to the police station to report the incident. Once at the police station, he couldn't decide whether or not he should go into the station or call home for a ride.

It was at this time he says the woman pulled up in a car with another man. Jerome claims he was not sure who this man was and decided he better leave, quick. He headed up the street to his sister's house and was arrested shortly thereafter. He told me he had not resisted arrest and was immediately sprayed with pepper spray. He claimed the can was emptied into his face. He further states he was left for 45 minutes on a bench, cuffed and shackled while the officers taunted him and called him racial slurs and a rapist.

Jerome says when the officers grabbed him they ripped his shirt. This is how he states the woman could identify his scar. He further stated there would be no DNA evidence, as he never touched the woman.

I wanted to believe him so badly. Strangely enough, the alleged victim never showed up at court. None of her friends or family members have ever shown up in court. I learned the alleged victim could not be located. She had given the police officers false information. She had a criminal history involving prostitution convictions. She also has a history of mental health issues. Neither the prosecutor, nor the defense attorney has ever been able to locate her.

Neither story rang totally true to me. I decided to believe in his innocence first and foremost. I had lived with him, in the same household for several years. He did not present as a person capable of such a crime. I stuck by him but remained cautious.

While in jail, I had learned Jerome had been the target of some of the gangs in the facility. Because of the nature of his alleged crime, he was a major target. There were threats on his life and he had been placed in protective custody for a period of time.

I began to start my campaign to bail Jerome out of jail. I asked God to make a way if he saw fit. Ironically, I was able to obtain the funds necessary to bail Jerome out of jail. It was purely an act of God. I had no resources and my credit had been shot. After the divorce, I had to file bankruptcy in order to get out of major debt. With this hanging over my head, I saw no way possible.

I attempted to take out an equity loan but figured this was a lost cause. I had already been denied once. I tried again and out of nowhere, the loan was approved. As a result of all of the repairs and updates made to the home by Jerome, the value on the home had increased close to $40,000 more than I had originally paid for it. Because of the seeds that he sowed by taking care of my home, the monies were available at a time when he needed it most. To this date, Jerome will confirm that he does not know why he did all of those things for me and repaired a home that wasn't his. He did it because his spirit kept compelling him to do it.

Two days after our scheduled wedding date, Jerome was released from jail on bail. I was really nervous about this but had resigned myself to the fact that if he messed up one time, I was gone for good. I had emphasized this fact to Jerome several times before he was released.

The next three months were fabulous. We attended church together and our relationship was overall pretty good. Jerome seemed to have taken a firm stance on serving God and staying out of the streets. There were anxious moments at times, but nothing significant. I noticed myself getting impatient. We started having small arguments about insignificant stuff.

My instincts were clueing me into the fact that something didn't feel right. This relationship was beginning to get stale for me and I constantly questioned whether or not I wanted to

VICTORIA A. ECKSTEIN

remain in it. I loved him, but felt as if I was living on the edge constantly. Wondering whether or not tonight would be the night he messed up.

Jerome would often talk about getting married. I definitely had no desire to get married. At least not to Jerome. I carried a lot of deep-seated anger and resentment towards him for all of the years I had tolerated his stuff. Some of my anger was directed at myself for believing in him and trusting him. I looked carefully at my situation and realized I was remaining in this situation because it was so much better than the last one. I started to resign myself to the fact that I was a wonderful woman. I would not continue to allow myself to take on someone else's issues and make them my own.

Granted, no one would provide perfection. There are always going to be issues in a relationship. There are some issues that are just not tolerable. This was a hard situation to deal with. Jerome was a wonderful man when he was on track and focused. But when he became frustrated, bored, or antsy, he was the worse. The good was so good, and it lulled me into remaining into the situation. His intolerable behaviors had changed so significantly that it provided hope that eventually things would continue to change. Jerome had made significant progress from the beginnings of our relationship. This is what kept me hooked. Unfortunately, this was also what was taking a tremendous toll on my emotional health.

I kept a copy of the police report of the incident in my briefcase. I would constantly take it out and read it over and over. Something didn't ring true. I learned the case had been dropped from superior court, where felonies are tried, to district court, where lesser offenses are tried. There was no DNA evidence, no grand jury indictments and no victim. Something didn't make sense to me.

All of this continues to be confusing. If Jerome were innocent, I still couldn't get past him being out on that night in

126

that particular area. Despite this, the Jerome I had known would never violate a woman like that. Deep down inside I knew this relationship was over. I knew there were unrevealed truths.

I decided it was only a matter of time. I would wait until the right time and then I would leave. The right time eventually came. It didn't exactly look like I wanted it to look, but it came nonetheless.

The day had gone by like any other. It was a pretty quiet day. Nicole had to work that evening until two o'clock in the morning. Jerome volunteered to pick her up from work. He rationalized this by stating it was really late for a woman to be out alone and he felt it would be safer for him to pick up my child from work.

Feeling pretty secure about this, I decided that would be great. I could get some much needed rest. I honestly didn't think it would be a problem. Besides, why would anyone with the type of criminal charges Jerome was facing desire to be out and into any kind of trouble?

I lay down at approximately 9:30 p.m. At about 10:00 p.m. I recall Jerome stating he was going drive to his mother's house to pick up a religious video. No big deal. He left and I went back to sleep. At approximately 12:30 p.m., I awoke abruptly. Wait a minute. Where was he?

I telephoned his mother. She stated he came there hours ago. He came into the house for 10 minutes, picked up the video and left. My mind began to race. This was definitely it for me. This was the last straw I had been waiting for. Part of me welcomed this closure and the other part felt sadness.

I paced the floor, once again. I watched the clock and practiced my speech. Two o'clock in the morning came and went. I was really upset now. Did he pick up my daughter? What was his condition? He had my car! It was 2:30 a.m. The telephone rang. It was him. I asked him where he had been. He lied and stated he left his mother's house and went straight to my daughter's job.

I let him know I had spoken to his mother and knew he was lying. He became upset and lied again, stating he was at his sister's house. I told him to bring my car and my daughter home right away. He hung up the phone on me. Twenty minutes later, I heard my car pull up.

This man then bolted up the stairs yelling and cursing. He flung his keys at me and began to destroy the room. Throwing things around and breaking things. He was cursing and yelling and I had managed to dial 911 and left the phone off of the hook. Nicole ran up the stairs upon hearing the commotion.

She got right up in his face and he became belligerent. She asked him if he had been drinking and he stated he had. He ripped the phone out of the wall. I ran past him and told my daughter to come on, NOW!! She didn't come immediately. I tried to call the police again from the telephone downstairs, but had no luck.

She came down the stairs and we ran out of the house to the car. He followed and stood outside the car, cursing and yelling. I sped off and got to the nearest pay phone as I had left my cell phone in the house. We called the police and informed them of the situation. I parked the car around the corner from the house with the lights off until I saw the police officers approach.

It seemed like forever before they arrived. Once they arrived, we pulled up to the house. My front door was wide open. The officers went into the house with flashlights and guns looking for Jerome. They were taken through the house to view the damage. He was nowhere around.

We gave them his picture and his mother's address. We told them of the charges he was facing. We were advised to leave the house for the night and they would call my cell phone once they had arrested him. The officer asked me if I wanted them to keep him locked up over the weekend. Over the weekend? That's it!

What good would that do me? We packed an overnight bag and left the house. I called the police station several times to see if he had been arrested. He had not been. The next morning, I went back to the house to assess the damage and clean my house.

During the course of my cleaning, I noticed the house keys were missing. I changed my locks and bought an anti-theft device for my car. I couldn't sleep and jumped at every single noise. I discovered he was back at his mother's house.

The aftermath was drama at its best. When he had first called, it was to inform me that I would lose the $5,000 as he was not going to show up for court. I decided not to let this form of manipulation influence my stance. I informed him that I could care less. I told him God had provided the money and if it was meant for me to have I would have it back. I further told him that I helped him out of the goodness of my heart when nobody else could. I later received a call stating he would show up for court.

He hasn't harassed or bothered me at my request. He apologized for his behavior but I had nothing to say. It was really over. Wow! God had spared me again. I thanked Him for whatever He was doing in my life.

I began to get another picture of Jerome. An outside source decided to inform me of the lifestyle Jerome had lived in Atlanta. It was hard to discern how much of this information was factual and how much of it was fabricated. The source from which the information derived was quite unreliable and had an ulterior motive for delivering the news.

Nevertheless, it became apparent that Jerome had been living a double life. Life with me seemed to be something he desperately wanted. He just couldn't get past his own inner demons. I felt liberated. I felt strong. I never cried.

Relationships will probably always be an area I struggle with. But I have grown so much throughout this last one. I can finally feel okay with being alone. I don't have a burning desire to go out and find someone or create situations I don't need to be a part of.

I was tired of wearing the label of victim. I wanted something positive to come out of my experiences. God has allowed me to become a survivor of incredible odds. My mother taught me early on to always seek the lesson in whatever hardship you endure.

The next three weeks following the break up, seemed to be a combination of mixed emotions. In one sense, I did not want Jerome out of my life completely because I cherished the goodness I saw in his heart. The other part of me wanted no part of him in my life because of all he had put me through. I felt greatly tempted to go find someone, anyone who would confirm for me my desirability as a woman. My self-esteem had been shot down, but only temporarily. I thought about temptation.

I was being strongly tempted to resort to old behavior. I thought about running to a nightclub and meeting some man, any man, to make me feel important. I resisted this negative thinking. My exposure to the goodness of God prevented me from going backwards. I compared resisting temptation to changing a normal sleeping position. At first it's uncomfortable and doesn't feel right. Resisting old patterns and temptation to go back to what is familiar is not a comfortable thing to do at first. But after some time, you begin to adjust. Eventually, you realize it's better for you not to return to that old sleeping position or your old ways.

During this brief three week period, I became totally focused on God. I began to see this situation in a totally different light. I could clearly see all of the manipulation, all of the lies, all of the deceit. I began to question myself. Did I hang in there so long because this appeared to be better than the last? Why was I willing to feed off of the crumbs he had tossed me here and there instead of eating nothing but a full course meal? Had I ever really learned the lesson? How could my life become a blessing for someone else? It is my hope and desire that this story will help someone else. If God can save me, he can save you.

Momma used to say, "God never gives you more than you can handle." I always thought, "How strong does He think I am? I don't think I can take any more." But each and every time, I have always had the strength to get through every storm, every battle.

Sure, underneath the outward surface, there lies a maze of scars and old wounds. As I carefully look at the patterns of my scars and wounds, I can see a picture emerge. A wonderful picture of a beautiful place. God has been preparing me for an incredible journey, leading me to a place of greatness. Everything God permits you to go through will ultimately be good for you. If you don't run away from it, it will strengthen you.

I decided it was time to write Jerome a letter. During a telephone conversation, he had expressed anger with me for not sticking with him throughout his struggles with his issues. He talked about everyone having issues and how people are quick to judge others without looking at themselves and their issues. He basically blamed me for not tolerating his mess. Hearing this infuriated me. I mustered up tremendous strength and wrote the following letter:

> Jerome:
> It blows my mind that you would have the absolute nerve to blame your mess on me. HOW DARE YOU!!!!!!! Your life is never going to change until you own up to your own mess. You can blame everyone else, or your addiction, or your issues (as you call it) or your choices if you want to. I guess that

makes you feel better. Well, it doesn't make me feel better.

There is no issue or addiction on this planet strong enough to compel your behind to go out and cheat with other women when you have a woman at home who loves you with all of her heart at home. You did that and you did that because you wanted to. PERIOD!

After speaking to you on the telephone, I decided to search through my journals to remind myself of exactly what kind of drama I have tolerated. When you first came into my life, I told you what this family had been through and what we did not want to go through again. You knew how traumatized we had been. YOU KNEW. You chose to lie about who you were and what you were about. You did this for your own selfish purposes. You fed me with half-truths and nonsense because according to you, if I knew everything I would have never given you a chance. That may or may not be true. Who knows. The point is, any decent person would have been honest and let the other person decide what they wanted to do. You never gave me that option.

My mistake was trusting you and believing in you. Lie after lie after lie. You slowly revealed your true self over time; or at least some of yourself. To this day, I am still learning about who you really are. Despite that, I honestly believed you wanted to change your life. So, I hung in there. I didn't want to be another person who didn't give you a chance, who walked away without allowing you the chance to change what you said you wanted to change. You, just like the others, mistook my kindness for weakness. BIG MISTAKE!

The first time you left for Atlanta you should have stayed gone. You knew who you were. I didn't. You would have saved me a lot of grief and pain. But NO ----- You told me you didn't want to come back and stay with your mother. You said you needed a place to stay. You said you loved me. You said you would be a different man. You said you wanted to be with me. You said you wanted this kind of life. You said you were tired of running. You said a lot of things. So, I let you stay here. You came into our home, our world, our lives. And you brought all of your crap with you.

Yes, things were chaotic when you first came into our lives. We had just gone through some horrible stuff. I hadn't even been divorced a year yet. I had major repair work to do. Granted, you helped me out tremendously. You did many kind things and were quite loving in your own way. You helped me clean up the mess and create some order in my life. I will never ever forget that and will always love you for that.

But what did you do? I can't forget the fact that you lived a double life and continually lied throughout our entire relationship. You consistently present this image of me and my children as people with tremendous issues. The difference between you and me is that I worked on my issues early on in the relationship. You constantly picked at trivial insignificant things in order to shift the focus off of all of your mess.

You can say whatever you want about Nicole or me or whoever. I don't care anymore. My daughter is doing better than most young ladies her age. So what, she has stuff to work on. That's expected of someone her age. She is still growing, still maturing, still

133

learning. I expect her to fall along the way.

In terms of the cigarettes you constantly bring up, I gave you the choice in the beginning of our relationship. I was honest. I told you I smoked. You could have left at any time, knowing you did not want a woman who smoked. You stayed. Your choice.

You, on the other hand, gave me minimal choices. You lied. I had to learn over the course of our life together just how deceitful you really are. You can't blame anyone else for not wanting to deal with your anger and violence. No one should have to put up with that kind of behavior. You are responsible for your behaviors. No one but you.

You want to be mad at me? Go ahead. Be mad. But take a close look at yourself. No one told you to lie about where you were and what you were doing. I told you I would not tolerate any more mess. No one told you to come home in a rage, cursing and swearing at the people you claim to love, because you don't like someone else not wanting to deal with any more of your stuff. Did everyone else make you break things, rip telephones out of the walls, throw keys, an electric heater, and an antique table at them?

And you definitely had no business touching my daughter. And don't even stoop low enough to deny it. I saw with my own eyes the scratches you left on her arm from you grabbing the phone out of her hand. You had no right pushing her head or slamming the closet door against her. You think that's acceptable? You think that's okay? My daughter had all the right in the world to try to protect her mother from your violence and abusive behaviors. What if it were your mother? Would you want to protect her from someone acting like they had just lost their mind, someone who might hurt her and is frightening her ----- again? You're damn right you would!

No, you didn't hit me. But what you did that night and many other nights is abusive. You think it's normal behavior to act that way and to frighten us over and over again in our own home until we have to run out in the night and call the police for protection from someone who is supposed to take care of us, supposed to love us and protect us? You would think a person facing all of the mess you're in right now would use better judgment and have better control over themselves. But, not you. That's crazy! What do you think this says to the legal system? It says you have anger issues and can be violent. Do you think this helps your case? Think again.

We have been together for three long years and six excruciating months. All of these years have been saturated with your mess, your drama. And it's not because you can't control yourself. That's bull! I've witnessed you control yourself for months at a time. You decided to step out because you wanted to, not because of any other reason. You decided to stop your self-destructive behaviors when you wanted to or you got tired of living this life you said you didn't want anymore. You have always had the ability to stay away from that lifestyle. You have always maintained a piece of that life because you haven't fully wanted to give it up. If you choose that life, you deal with the consequences that come along with it. Look at all of the progress you have made when you have decided not to indulge in that type of life. Then look at all of the destruction that life has caused in your life. You decide what is better. If you like that drama or need that chaos in your life, then keep it. But don't expect anybody else to want it and don't get mad if someone else decides they don't need it.

You have hurt me so badly. This pain is the worse pain I have ever endured in my life. I did not deserve this. I will never allow anyone to play me for a fool again. You talk to me as if I shouldn't be affected by your cheating. How can I not be hurt and affected by it. It's no big deal to you because I never hurt you like that. I've never disrespected you that way. Of course, you're okay. No big deal, right? Wrong. It is a big deal. This has been devastating for me. But why should you care? You don't have to picture in your mind, me with another man. That's my burden to bear. Picturing you with not one, but many other woman.

You complain to whoever you want to listen about my smoking and Nicole's struggles or whatever you want to call it. Big Deal ---- oooooh! Let's see, what do I have to complain about? I only have loved a man who cheats on me, lies to me, curses me out when things don't go his way, a man who brings trashy, stankin' woman to my house, a man who ruins the one and only vacation I have ever had in my life, leaves drugs in my house, can't be trusted, messes up my car, doesn't come home at night, leaves condoms and Playboy magazines in a car he just had another woman in, breaks things up, throws things at me, scares me and my daughter out of our own home, brings trifling folks to my house and around my teenage daughters, gets high ever couple of months, leaves cocaine residue and alcohol spills in my car, scratches up my car, has strange women in my bedroom, brings strangers into my home to get high and leaves them alone in my home while I am recovering in the hospital from major surgery, gets arrested over and over again (for some reason that usually involves another woman), gets arrested for an unspeakable crime three weeks before our wedding date, a man who shouldn't have been out that night in the first place especially in an area known for drugs and prostitutes, ------ the list goes on and on and on.

No, our issues are not the same. Believe that! Yes, everyone has issues, but you have major issues that keep repeating themselves over and over again. Issues that should never be inflicted on anyone else, especially someone you claim to love. Especially someone who tried to love you, someone who opened her already broken heart to you as well as allowed you into her home and her children's lives.

I refuse to let you or anyone else treat me like trash and blame me for it. That hurts beyond measure. It's bad enough these things existed in the first place, but to blame me or my child. That's an awful thing to do to someone. I will not allow you to try to shift this again. You caused this, not me.

Sure, Jerome, you can go out there and find another woman. You're a good-looking man with a wonderful personality. Besides, you've been with other women throughout our entire relationship anyway. There's nothing new there. One day you will see that all of that is just superficial and can never satisfy you or anyone else. Anyone can have their body temporarily pleased. But, the real satisfaction comes from having a meaningful relationship with someone who truly loves you. It's hard to find someone who can fulfill the needs of your heart. Women like me are hard to find. How many women do you think are out there who will love you no matter what you look like? How many will love you broke and broke down? How many woman will have the ability to see beyond the rough edges and recognize what's underneath, what's inside? I took you as you were and loved you despite your shortcomings. You took full advantage of that, didn't you? Thanks.

I guess you're happy with yourself and are feeling quite justified for causing so much pain and trauma in my life. I admire your ability to look in the mirror everyday and feel good about what you did and still live peacefully within yourself, blaming it all on us.

But that's okay. I have strength that is God given. No one can take it away from me. God sees me for what I am worth. God has kept and protected me throughout it all. God has kept me sane throughout incredible odds. God has given me guidance and direction. God has loved me and will continue to love me even if you don't.

I hope you can continue to find peace within yourself and can continue to live with yourself, not fully accepting responsibility for you own actions. Because I will live the rest of my life knowing I DID NOT deserve this and I am worth so much more.

Signed,
Cracked But Not Broken

I felt so much better after writing that letter. The letter itself sounded a bit immature and was more my way of releasing some anger and stress. It felt good knowing I stopped allowing myself to get sucked into someone else's mess and feeling at fault for things I could not control. I'm not sure what I will do with the letter. Writing it was gratifying enough. Did I care if he read it? Not really. I had no point to prove. Jerome knew everything he had done. It wasn't about the words. Talk is cheap. It's about my own actions and reactions to the situation that mattered. It was time for me to love myself first. I felt comfort in knowing God has loved me throughout all of this. I wanted to share my triumph with the world. I wanted everyone to know how good God has been to me.

It is not my intent to push God on anyone. Besides, that is the biggest way to turn people off. No one likes to be pushed. Not even me. It is my feeling that by exposing others to the goodness of God it will at least open the door for curiosity. Ask yourself, who is this God? Can he help me?

You can take anyone to a well but you can't force them to drink the water. All you can do is expose them to the quench water provides. Many times, people aren't thirsty enough. Or they sip just enough to keep them satisfied. Not realizing, you can take sips here and there, but eventually your body will need more. At some point in time, our bodies will have a strong thirst for water. This usually happens when we have gone without water for a while and our bodies go through some type of ailment. Our desire for the strength the water provides increases.

Compare our need for water with our need for God. We replace water with other forms of liquids, such as juices, coffee, etc. These may quench us for the moment or taste sweet and pleasing to our palates. But they can never replace the fulfillment of the water.

We all need God in our lives. We replace God with other worldly things that make us feel good. Our lives go on without major incidents for periods of time. We think we don't need God or maybe just a little bit of God. That is, until we have a major crisis. That is usually the time when people diligently seek out his help.

We fill up on versions of water that contain additives or artificial sweeteners. This can keep us going for quite awhile. Compare this to what superficially sustains us in life. We run to things that please us, make us feel good and temporarily serve our fleshly purposes. These things are not necessarily good for us and in time come with consequences. In time, we will be seeking the sweetness and the purity of the water.

Nothing can replace God and how he can take care of your every need. As with water, God is good for us. What is it that both God and water can do for you. Drinking water on a daily basis makes our skin look better, our outside appearance healthier. It flushes out impurities and gives us strength when we are feeling weak. Without water, we will die. It is life sustaining.

God can become your living water. He can flush out the bad and replace it with the good. He can give you strength, make you look and feel better. But most importantly, He can sustain your life.

All you have to do is drink daily. Seek Him daily. Rely on Him. Things won't change overnight. Everything has to go through a process. But in time, progress will start to show. Give God the highest praise whenever you can.

I take comfort in the fact that I am not where I used to be. I'm not pretending to be problem free or totally healed. I am still working through the process. But I am growing stronger and wiser. I am constantly seeking the quench of God's living water.

Thank Him for the little things you take for granted, like waking up to see another day. Stop asking God for material things and ask Him for strength and wisdom to guide you through your life; to give you insight as to your journey's purpose.

Most importantly, trust God with all of your heart. Don't depend on your thinking. We have a way of justifying things, of creating scenarios to satisfy our own desires. Inside our spirits are churning because we know something is not right. Ask God to help you distinguish between his divine will and your own worldly desires. Are you moving in His direction or you own?

I will never forget Jerome. I will always love the man that he allowed me to see. I feel saddened at the loss of him in my life. I don't believe he set out to hurt me. But I realize I can't expect two incomplete people to come together and have a successful relationship. In a relationship, both individuals need to be whole human beings, with a strong sense of love for self. Neither needs to rely on the other to make them feel complete as a human being. That is a sure-fire recipe for disaster.

I have decided to patiently wait for God to move in my life and not to create my own scenarios and blame their failures on God. God presented me with all of the signs I needed to leave this situation long time ago. Instead, I kept justifying what was happening (not on a conscious level) in order to avoid being without the good things Jerome gave me.

I am now alone and loving it! I am not crawling out of my own skin trying to surround myself with people to avoid myself. I value my time for myself. I am not opposed to marriage or relationships. As a matter of fact, I look forward to the day when God decides it's time for me to have somebody. While I'm waiting, I plan on being very productive with my time.

I have two daughters to spend quality time with and a beautiful granddaughter. I have time to get closer to God and listen for his direction without distraction. I no longer need to seek the approval of others to validate who I am as a person. I love me. I am one of God's creations. God doesn't make junk. God is top notch and creates quality pieces of art. I am one of the many masterpieces in God's gallery.

Learn from my mistakes. Don't create your own plan in life. Look for God's plan for your life. Seek His divine will. Let Him direct you as to where you are supposed to go. Rely on Him totally, even if it hurts. If letting go of a relationship hurts

141

so bad you can't see straight, ask God to help you. It may be the best thing for you. It may be God's way of moving someone out of your life to bring something in that is better suited for you.

Maybe you were in that person's life for a purpose. The purpose of the relationship may have been served and the time to move on is now. Maybe, just maybe, God has some work to do in that other person's life before He can allow a relationship or marriage to happen. Maybe God is working on you as well. Maybe God is saving you from a life of pure hell.

Whatever God is doing in your life, trust in His plan, His wisdom, His power. Hold your head up high in the midst of your anguish and shout *HALLELUJAH ANYHOW!*

Printed in the United States
19194LVS00001B/374

9 781413 706574